OXFORD PROGRESSIVE ENGLISH READERS

General Editor: D. H. Howe

You Only Live Twice

You Only Live Twice

by IAN FLEMING

HONG KONG

OXFORD UNIVERSITY PRESS

KUALA LUMPUR SINGAPORE JAKARTA TOKYO

Oxford University Press

OXFORD LONDON GLASGOW
NEW YORK TORONTO MELBOURNE WELLINGTON
KUALA LUMPUR SINGAPORE JAKARTA HONG KONG TOKYO
DELHI BOMBAY CALCUTTA MADRAS KARACHI
NAIROBI DAR ES SALAAM CAPE TOWN

ISBN 0 19 581085 6

This reader is adapted from
YOU ONLY LIVE TWICE
first published 1964
© Glidrose Productions Ltd. 1964
Adaptation published 1978
by arrangement with Jonathan Cape Ltd.
Second impression 1979

Retold by Rosemary Border. Illustrated by Tomaz Mok. Simplified according to
the language grading scheme especially compiled by D.H. Howe

Printed by Windmill Printing Co. 8 Shipyard Lane, Wah Ha Fty. Bldg. H.K.
Published by Oxford University Press, News Building, North Point, Hong Kong

Contents

Oxford Progressive English Readers Language Scheme

The OPER language grading scheme was especially compiled by D. H. Howe as a guide to the preparation of language teaching material for school pupils and adults learning English as a second or foreign language. The scheme provides lists of words and language structures subdivided into three grades of difficulty and meant to be used in conjunction with each other.

The items were chosen according to two main principles: first, that they are likely to have been learnt or at least encountered *before* the stage indicated; second, that they are frequently occurring and useful, necessary to express a wide range of ideas, and difficult to replace with simpler words or constructions.

Use of the scheme is intended to eliminate unnecessary difficulties of language which would otherwise hinder understanding and enjoyment.

1 Scissors Cut Paper

The *geisha* called 'Trembling Leaf' knelt in front of James
Bond and gave him a small cup of *sake*. The short strong man
sitting at the low red table opposite Bond leaned forward.

'Bondo-san,' said Tiger Tanaka, who was Head of the Japanese Secret Service, 'I will now challenge you to this foolish   5
game, and I promise you that you will not win.' The big
brown face, that Bond had come to know so well in the past
month, split in a wide smile. Bond knew that smile. It wasn't
a friendly smile.

Bond laughed. 'All right, Tiger. But first, more *sake*! And   10
not in these silly little cups. Is there such a thing as an ordinary large glass in some corner behind your Ming vases?'

'Bondo-san, Ming is Chinese. Your knowledge of such
things is poor and your drinking habits are disgusting. We
have a saying about *sake*. "The man drinks the first jug of   15
sake, then the second jug drinks the first; then it is the *sake*
that drinks the man." '

Tiger turned to Trembling Leaf. She bowed low and left
the room. Tiger turned to Bond. 'You have gained her respect,
Bondo-san. Few men can drink *sake* in these quantities with-   20
out showing it.'

The *geisha* party had been going on for two hours, and
Bond's jaws were aching with polite smiles. He knew that
Tiger Tanaka was observing his efforts too.

'*Geisha* parties,' Dikko Henderson had warned him, 'aren't   25
much fun for a foreigner. But Tiger is doing you a great
honour. The party will cost him a small fortune, so look
happy! It might make all the difference between success and
failure for you.'

So now Bond smiled, accepted a large glass of *sake* and   30
drank it down very quickly. Then he banged his fist on the
low red table. Pretending to be fierce, he said, 'All right,

Tiger! Let's go!'

It was the old game of Scissors cut Paper, Paper wraps Stone, Stone blunts Scissors. Children play it all over the world. The fist is the Stone, two fingers are the Scissors, and
5   a flat hand is the Paper. The game consists of guessing which the other person will choose, and of you yourself choosing one that will defeat him.

Tiger Tanaka rested his fist on the table opposite Bond. The two men looked carefully into each other's eyes. There
10   was silence. Suddenly this became more than a children's game. Should I try to win this foolish game, thought Bond, or should I try to lose? But it was just as difficult to lose on purpose as to win. Oh, does it really matter? thought Bond. Then he had a nasty feeling that this foolish little game mat-
15   tered very much.

Here was Tiger Tanaka, with his Oxford education and his knowledge of the West. But Bond saw the hard glitter in the dark eyes. The man was serious.

Since Bond had arrived in Japan he had carefully practised
20   sitting with his legs crossed. Dikko Henderson advised it.

'With these people,' he had said, 'you'll spend a lot of time sitting on the ground. There's only one way to do it — that's in the Indian position, with your legs crossed and the sides of your feet on the floor. It hurts a lot. It takes a bit of practice,
25   but you'll gain their respect.' Bond had more or less learnt the art, but now, after two hours, his knee-joints felt as if they were on fire. He said to Tiger, 'Playing against a master such as you, I must first adopt a more relaxed position, to help me to think more clearly.' He got painfully to his feet, stretched and
30   sat down again — this time with one leg under the low table and his left elbow resting on the bent knee of the other. It was a great relief. He lifted his glass for Trembling Leaf to fill, drank the *sake* quickly, and suddenly crashed his right fist down on the table. He looked fiercely at Tiger Tanaka. 'Right!'
35   Tiger bowed. Bond bowed back. Tiger's eyes looked into Bond's, trying to read his plan. Bond had decided to have no plan.

'Three games of three?' said Tiger.

'Right.'

The two fists rose slowly from the table-top, and shot forward. Tiger kept his fist in the Stone position. Bond's palm
5 was open in the Paper that wrapped the Stone. One to Bond.
Again the moment of truth. Tiger kept the Stone. Bond's
first and second fingers were open in the Scissors. Tiger's
Stone blunted them. One each.

Next time Tiger kept his Stone. Bond wrapped it with his
10 Paper. First game to Bond.

The second game took longer. They both kept showing the
same thing, which meant playing again. It was as if the two
men were trying to read each other's minds. But that could
not be true, since Bond had no plan. It was just luck. Tiger
15 won the game. One game each.

Last game! The two men looked at each other. A gleam of
red shone in the depths of Tiger's dark eyes. Bond saw it.
Shall I try to lose? he asked himself. But he won the game,
blunting Tiger's Scissors with his Stone, and wrapping Tiger's
20 Stone with his Paper.

Tiger bowed low. Bond bowed even lower. He looked for
something polite to say.

'I must get this game adopted in time for the Olympic
Games!'
25 Tiger Tanaka laughed with controlled politeness. 'You play
well. What was the secret of your method?'

Bond had had no method. He quickly invented one. 'You
are a man of rock and steel, Tiger,' he said politely. 'I guessed
that the paper would be the thing you used the least.'
30 Tiger Tanaka accepted this polite nonsense. He bowed.
Bond bowed also, and drank more *sake.* 'To you, Tiger,' he
said, and lifted his glass.

'Bondo-san,' said Tiger, 'I have matters to discuss with
you. Will you do me the honour of coming to my house for a
35 drink?'

According to Dikko, it was an unusual honour to be invited to a Japanese private house. So, thought Bond, I did right to win that game. This may mean great things! Bond bowed low. 'Nothing could give me more pleasure, Tiger,' he said aloud.

An hour later, to Bond's relief, they were sitting in chairs with a drink-tray between them. The lights of Yokohama *5* glowed in the distance, and a slight smell of the sea came in through the wide-open partition which led to the garden. The three other partitions in the square room were also open, showing a bedroom, a small study and a passage.

Tiger had opened the partitions when they entered the *10* room.

'In the West,' he said, 'when you have secrets to discuss, you shut all the doors and windows. In Japan, we throw everything open, to make sure that no one can listen at the thin walls. And what I have to discuss with you now is very *15* secret indeed. Is the *sake* warm enough for you? Are these the cigarettes you prefer? Then listen to what I have to say to you, and swear on your honour never to tell anyone.' Tiger Tanaka laughed his unpleasant laugh. 'If you break your promise, I will kill you.' *20*

2   Bond's Last Case?

Exactly one month before, M. was entertaining a guest for lunch at his club. The waiter came with the cigars. He offered them to M.'s guest, Sir James Molony. Sir James lit his cigar with care. Then he took a drink of brandy and sat back. He
5 said, 'All right, my friend. What's the problem?'

M.'s mind was elsewhere. He seemed to be having difficulty in lighting his pipe. 'What problem?' he said.

Sir James Molony was the greatest brain surgeon in England. The year before, he had won a Nobel prize for his work.
10 He was consulted often by the Secret Service. He said, 'My friend, like everybody else, you have certain patterns of behaviour. One of them consists of asking me to lunch with you, and then telling me some awful secret and asking me to help you with it. What do you want this time?'

15 M. looked at him coldly. 'It's 007. I'm getting more and more worried about him.'

'You've read my two reports on him. What's new?'

'Nothing. He's just the same — going slowly downhill. He comes to work late, makes mistakes, drinks too much, spends
20 too much. One of my best men, too. I can hardly believe it.'

Sir James Molony shook his head. 'I can. You either don't read my reports or you don't pay enough attention to them. That man is suffering from shock.' Sir James leaned forward. 'You're a hard man, M. In your job you have to be. But there
25 are some human problems that you just can't solve that way. Here's this agent of yours, tough and brave, and unmarried. Then he suddenly falls in love. He marries her and within a few hours that criminal shoots her dead. What was his name?'

'Blofeld,' said M., 'Ernst Stavro Blofeld.'

30 'All right. And your man only got a knock on the head. Nothing wrong with him, except shock. He told me that he had lost all his interest in his work, even in life. I hear this

sort of talk from patients every day. In your man's case what caused it was the loss of a loved one, made worse by the fact that he blamed himself for her death. My friend, that is a terrible burden for anybody. I thought, and I said so in my report, that his job, with all its dangers, would shake him out 5 of this state. Have you tried him on any tough cases in the last few months?'

'Two,' said M. in a flat voice. 'He made a mess of both of them.'

'So what are you going to do about it?' 10

'Dismiss him,' said M. fiercely. 'I've got no room for a man who makes mistakes. He'll get sick-pay, of course.' M. looked into the clear, blue, understanding eyes of the famous doctor. 'You do see my point, James,' he said. 'There's just nowhere I can put 007 so that he won't cause harm.' 15

'You'll be losing one of your best men.'

'He used to be. He isn't now.'

Sir James Molony looked out of the window and thought carefully. He made up his mind. 'Give him one more chance, M.' 20

'What sort of chance?'

'Well, have you got something really awkward, some hopeless case that you can give this man? Something that's terribly important but looks impossible. What he needs most of all is something that'll really make him sweat, something that will 25 force him to forget his personal troubles. Give him something that really matters to his country. It may help him. Anyway, give him the chance.'

That afternoon, the urgent ring of the red telephone, that had been silent for so many weeks, sent Mary Goodnight out 30 of her seat like a bullet from a gun.

'Yes, sir. No, sir. It's his secretary speaking.' She looked down at her watch, knowing the worst.

'It's most unusual, sir. I'm sure he'll be here soon. Shall I ask him to call you, sir?' 35

She noticed that her hand was trembling. 'Oh, James!' she thought angrily, 'where are you?' She said aloud, 'Oh,

James, please hurry.' She walked sadly back and sat down at
her empty typewriter.

The state of your health, the weather, the wonders of
nature — these things rarely bother a man before he reaches
5   the middle thirties. It is a sign of middle age when they do.

Until this year, James Bond had never noticed any of these
things. He had always had good health. The weather was just
a question of what to wear. As for birds, bees and flowers
and the wonders of nature, it only mattered if they bit or
10   stung, and whether they smelt good or bad. But today, just
eight months after Tracy's death, James Bond was sitting in
Queen Mary's Rose Garden in Regent's Park, and his mind
was full of just these things.

First his health. He felt ill, and knew that he also looked
15   ill. For months, without telling anyone, he had been looking
for a doctor to make him feel better. He told them, 'I feel ill.
I sleep badly. I eat almost nothing. I drink too much, and my
work is suffering. Make me better.' And each man did tests,
asked him questions, and told him there was nothing wrong
20   with him. Now here he was in this quiet garden. He looked at
his watch. Just after three o'clock, he thought. Due back at
two-thirty. My God, he thought, it's hot. He wiped his hand
across his forehead. I never used to sweat like this, he said to
himself. I wish I could have a holiday, bathe whenever I
25   want. But I've had my holiday for this year. That awful
month in Jamaica after Tracy died. I don't want to go
through another month like that again. It's all right here, really. Lovely roses. They smell good too. Nice noise of bees,
distant traffic. Oh, well, I'd better go back and face Mary.
30   She's right to be angry with me for staying out so late. James
Bond got to his feet and walked slowly towards the office.
Three-thirty, he thought. Only two more hours to go before
the next drink.

The man in the lift said, 'Your secretary's rather worried,
35   sir. She's been asking everywhere for you.'

Bond walked along the quiet passage to the door marked
'007'. Mary Goodnight looked up at him and said calmly, 'M.

wants you. He telephoned half an hour ago.'

'Who's M.?'

Mary Goodnight jumped to her feet. Her eyes flashed. 'Oh, James, stop it! Your hair's a mess. Here, use my comb.' Bond took the comb and ran it through his hair. 'Please, James,' 5 she continued, and her eyes were bright. 'Go to him. Perhaps it's something important. Something exciting.' She made a desperate effort to put encouragement into her voice.

'It's always exciting starting a new job. I'm finished in this one, anyway.' 10

She turned away and put her hands up to her face. He patted her on the shoulder and picked up the red telephone, '007 here, sir.'

'I'm sorry, sir. Had to go to the dentist.' And then, 'I know, sir. I'm sorry. I left it in my desk.' He put the tele- 15 phone down slowly. He looked round his office as if saying goodbye to it, walked out and along the passage like a man going to his death.

Miss Moneypenny, M.'s secretary, looked up at him in an unfriendly way. 'You can go in.' 20

Bond squared his shoulders and looked at the polished wood door behind which so many exciting cases had begun. He reached for the door handle almost as if he expected it to give him an electric shock. He turned it, walked through and closed the door behind him. 25

3　The Impossible Mission

M. was standing by the big window looking out across the park. Without looking round he said, 'Sit down.' No name, no number!

Bond took his usual place opposite M.'s tall chair. He no-
5　ticed that there were no papers on the red leather desk-top. And the In and Out baskets were both empty. Suddenly he felt really bad about everything. The empty desk, the empty chair, were the final accusation. We have nothing for you, they seemed to say. You're no use to us any more.

10　M. came over and sat down. He looked at Bond. 'You know why I've sent for you?' he said.

'I can guess, sir. You can have my resignation.'

'What *are* you talking about?' said M. angrily. 'It's not your fault that your team's been idle for so long. That's the
15　way things go.'

'But I made a mess of the last two jobs. And I know my health's been poor these last few months.'

'Nonsense. You've been through a bad time, that's all. As for your last two missions, anyone can make mistakes. But I
20　can't have idle hands around the place, so I'm taking you out of the Double-0 department.'

Bond's heart sank. The old man was being kind, trying to let him down lightly. Bond said, 'Then I'd still like to resign, sir. I've had my Double-0 number for too long. I'm not in-
25　terested in other work.'

M. lifted his right fist and banged it down on the desk.

'Who do you think you're talking to? I sent for you to give you promotion and the most important mission you've ever had, and you talk to me about resignation! Young fool!'

30　Bond was amazed and excited. What was all this about? He said, 'I'm sorry, sir. I thought I'd been doing badly lately.'

'I'll soon tell you when you're doing badly.' M. banged the

desk again, but less hard. 'Now listen to me. I'm giving you
promotion to the Foreign Office Department, a four-figure
number, and extra pay. You can keep your present office and
your secretary, if you like. In fact, I'd prefer it. I want to
keep your change of duty secret. Understand?'   *5*

'Yes, sir.'

'In any case, you'll be leaving for Japan in a few days.
Chief of Staff is arranging everything himself. Not even my
secretary knows about it. As you can see,' M. pointed to the
empty desk, 'there aren't even any papers on the case. That's   *10*
how important it is.'

'But why have you chosen me, sir?' Bond's heart was beating fast.

'For the simple reason that the job's impossible. No, not
exactly. Let's say you're most unlikely to succeed. You've   *15*
done well in such missions in the past. If you succeed in this
one, which I very much doubt, you will double our information about the Soviet Union.'

'Can you tell me some more about it, sir?'

'I'll have to, as there's nothing written down. Well now.   *20*
You know a bit about codes?'

'Very little, sir. I've preferred to avoid the subject, in case
the enemy ever caught me.'

'Quite right. Well, the Japanese are extremely clever with
codes. Since the war, with American help, they've built some   *25*
amazing code-breaking machines. And for the last year
they've been reading all the Soviet material.'

'That's wonderful, sir,'

'Not for us. The Americans aren't passing it on!'

'Oh . . . What's my job, sir?'   *30*

'There's a man in Tokyo called Tiger Tanaka. Head of their
Secret Service. He's an interesting man — went to Oxford before the war. Well, he's the man in control of the information
we want. You must go out there and get it from him. How, I
don't know. That's up to you. But you can see why I say   *35*
you're unlikely to succeed.

'You'll be working under the Australians. We haven't had

an office there since 1950. They tell me the Australian
agent's a good man. Will you have a try, James?'
    M.'s face was suddenly friendly. It wasn't friendly often.
James Bond felt that there were things hidden behind this
5 mission, things he didn't understand. Was M. giving him his
last chance? But he said, 'Yes, sir. I'll try.'
    'Good.' M. leaned forward and lifted the telephone. 'Chief
of Staff? What number have you given 007? Right. He's
coming to see you now.'
10   M. leaned back and gave another of his rare smiles. 'You've
kept part of your old number. All right, 7777. Go along and
see the Chief of Staff.'
    'Yes, sir and —er — thank you.' Bond got up and walked
over to the door and let himself out. He walked over to M.'s
15 secretary, Miss Moneypenny, and kissed her on the cheek. 'Be
an angel, Penny,' he said, 'and telephone Mary Goodnight.
Tell her I'm going to take her out to dinner tonight! A special
occasion!'
    'Oh? What?'
20   'Oh, I don't know. The Queen's birthday or something.'
James Bond crossed the room and went into the Chief of
Staff's office.
    Miss Moneypenny picked up her telephone and passed the
message to Mary Goodnight in an excited voice. She said, 'I
25 really think he's all right again, Mary. He's just like he used to
be. I don't know what M.'s said to him, but he had lunch
with Sir James Molony today. Don't tell James that. But it
may have something to do with it. He's with the Chief of
Staff. And Bill said, "Do not disturb". So it sounds like some
30 sort of job. Bill was very mysterious about it.'
    Bill Tanner, Bond's best friend in the Service, looked up
and smiled. 'Sit down, James,' he said. 'So you've agreed to
this hopeless mission?'
    'It's hopeless, all right,' Bond said cheerfully. 'This man
35 Tanaka sounds a difficult case, and I'm no good at anything
diplomatic. Now tell me, how am I going to do it? Have I got
anything to offer Tanaka in exchange for his code-breaking?'

'He can have everything from our station in Hong Kong. Offer him the Macao "Blue Route" — he may want that.

'Now, the man in Tokyo is an Australian called Richard Henderson — Dikko to his friends. You'll have an Australian passport and you'll go out as his assistant. That'll make the *5* Japanese respect you. If you get the information, Henderson will push it back to us through Melbourne.'

'Very well. I'll go and start learning about the mysterious East!'

'Good luck, James.'   *10*

'Welcome!' said the pretty air-hostess of Japan Air Lines. It was a week later, and James Bond was sitting in the comfortable seat of the big aeroplane at London Airport. When it reached 30,000 feet, Bond ordered his first drink and decided to enjoy this impossible mission.   *15*

4 Dikko Henderson

The huge right first crashed into the left palm with a noise like a gun. The great square face of the Australian turned almost purple. Bond said mildly, 'Relax, Dikko. What's the matter?'

5 Richard Lovelace Henderson, of Her Majesty's Australian Diplomatic Service, looked fiercely round the small bar and said out of the corner of his large and usually cheerful mouth, 'You stupid Englishman, they've been listening to us! That pig Tanaka's put a microphone under the table. See the little

10 wire down the table leg? And see that man by the bar in the blue suit? That's one of Tiger's men.'

'Well, if Mr Tanaka's listening in, he'll hear some interesting things from you!'

'You're right, he will!' said Dikko Henderson. 'But he al-

15 ready knows what I think of him. Now he'll just have it in writing! Well, hear me now, Tiger!' He raised his voice. 'I hope your rice sticks in your throat tomorrow.'

Bond laughed. He remembered his first sight of Dikko at the airport. The huge man in the grey suit had held out an

20 enormous hand.

'Glad to meet you. I'm Henderson. As you were the only Englishman on the plane, I guessed you must be Bond. Here, give me your bag. I've got a car outside. Let's get away from this mad-house!'

25 Henderson looked like a retired boxer. He had a lined, friendly brown face, rather hard blue eyes, and a badly broken nose. He was sweating freely. Bond followed him to a smart car which was waiting in a no-parking area. The driver got out and bowed. Henderson gave him his instructions in

30 Japanese and followed Bond into the back seat.

'I'm taking you to your hotel first — the Okura. Then we'll do some serious drinking. Have you had dinner?'

'About six of them, as far as I can remember. The Japanese Air Lines certainly take care of your stomach.'

Bond looked at the city through which they were passing.

'Doesn't look the most attractive city in the world. And why are we driving on the left?'   5

'Who knows? The Japanese do lots of things the wrong way round. Light switches go up instead of down. Taps turn to the left. But you soon get used to it. But Tokyo's awful. It's either too hot or too cold, or raining. And the earth moves nearly every day. But don't worry about that. It just 10 makes you feel slightly drunk. The big storms are worse. If one starts to blow, just go into the most solid-looking bar you can see, and have a few drinks. The first ten years are the worst!

'It's very expensive if you insist on having Western-style 15 things, but I stick to the back streets and do all right. But you must know the language for that, and know when to bow and take off your shoes and so on. You'll have to learn the basic things fast, James, if you want to make any progress with the people that you've come to see.' Henderson spoke in 20 Japanese to the driver, who was looking in his driving-mirror. The driver laughed and replied cheerfully. 'Thought so,' said Henderson. 'Somebody's following us — one of Tanaka's men. I told him where you were staying, but he wants to make sure for himself. Don't worry. It's just his way.'   25

And now Dikko Henderson reached under the table and pulled out the microphone wires. He left them hanging. 'Now then, James, to business. I've arranged for you to meet Tiger tomorrow morning at eleven. Now, I don't know what you're here for, and I don't want to know. But I know that you 30 want to get some important information out of Tiger without the Americans knowing. Right? Well, good luck.'

'But what sort of man is this Tanaka?' asked Bond. 'Is he your enemy or your friend?'

'Both. More of a friend probably. We've got things in com- 35 mon. I've managed to keep him out of two marriages. So he's grateful to me. This is a very important part of Japanese life.

When you owe somebody a favour, you aren't very happy until you have paid it back. And if a man makes you a present of a box of chocolates, you mustn't pay him back with a smaller one. It's got to be an equally large one — larger
5 if possible — then *he* will owe *you* a favour.

'Well now, Tiger owes me a very big favour. He's paid little slices of it off with various bits of secret information. He's paid off another big slice by accepting your presence here and agreeing to see you so soon after your arrival. He some-
10 times makes ordinary people wait weeks. He is likely to try to do what you want because that will pay off the favour that he owes me, and make *me* owe *him* one . . . Oh, you'll soon get the idea. Now let's go and have dinner.'

5　The Code-Breaking Machine

Dikko Henderson came for Bond at ten o'clock next morning.
'Come on, let's go. We mustn't keep Tiger waiting. I once
did and he didn't speak to me for a week.'

It was a normal Tokyo day in late summer. They drove for
half an hour towards Yokohama and stopped outside a grey   *5*
building with 'All Asia Tourist Board' on the wall. Dikko led
the way through an entrance hall with books and postcards
on sale, then through a door marked 'International Relations'.
As they walked on, Dikko said quietly, 'Up to this point, the
people here really were working for the Tourist Board. Tiger's   *10*
department starts here.' Behind a wall of book-shelves a small
door was hidden. It was marked, 'Danger! Work in progress.'
From behind it came the noise of building work. Dikko
walked through the door. The room was empty. There was
no sign of building work. Dikko laughed at Bond's surprise.   *15*
He pointed to a large metal box on the back of the door.
'Recorded noises,' he said. 'Clever, isn't it? It sounds just like
the real thing. And this floor is a specially noisy one. Nobody
can cross it without making a noise.' Sure enough, the wood-
en floor creaked when they walked across it. The door at the   *20*
other side of the room opened and Bond saw a short, square
man sitting at a small table reading a book. It was a tiny, box-
like room, with only one door. Dikko spoke to the man in
Japanese. Bond heard the words 'Tanaka-san.' The man
bowed. Dikko turned to Bond. 'You're on your own now.   *25*
Good luck!'

Bond walked into the tiny room. The door closed behind
him. There was a row of buttons beside the desk, and the
man pushed one of them. The room was a lift. The mysterious
East, thought Bond. Whatever next?   *30*

They went down for some time. When the lift stopped, the
guard opened the door. Bond stepped out and stood still. He

was standing on the platform of an underground station!
There it was — the red and green lights, the tunnels, the
empty cigarette-machine in the wall beside him! And a man
came out of the cigarette-machine. It was another secret
5 door. The man said, in good English, 'Please come this way,
sir.'

Bond went through the door. The short, square, strong
man came forward across the handsome red carpet and held
out his hand. 'My dear Mr Bond. Good morning. It is a great
10 pleasure to meet you. How do you like my offices? Rather

different from your own chief's, no doubt. But the new underground station will take ten years to finish, and there is not much office space in Tokyo. This station is quiet. It is private. It is also cool. I shall be sorry when the trains run at
5 last and we move out.'

Bond said, 'It's a brilliant idea. And I enjoyed the Tourist Board too.'

Tiger Tanaka laughed. His gold teeth glittered under the hard white lights. 'Do you smoke?' James Bond took a
10 cigarette and lit it.

'Tell me, Mr Bond,' Tiger Tanaka went on, 'what are your views on Japan? Have you been enjoying yourself so far?'

'I am sure one always enjoys oneself with Dikko Henderson.'

15 'Yes. He is a good friend of mine. I enjoy his company. We have some tastes in common.'

'I suspect he is lonely,' said Bond. 'Can't you find a nice Japanese girl for him?'

'I have arranged for him to meet many, without results so
20 far. But tell me, Mr Bond, we are not here to discuss Mr Henderson's private life. What can I do for you?'

Bond smiled. 'I need the information from your code-breaking machine.'

'Our code machine! Ah, yes, I am sure your country wants
25 it very much. Here is an example of what it can do.' Tiger Tanaka opened a drawer in his desk and took out some papers. He passed a typewritten sheet to Bond. 'Do you promise on your word of honour not to tell anyone about this?'
30 'I do.'

The message was in English. The Russians, it seemed, were preparing to threaten to bomb Britain, to make America remove her soldiers and weapons from Europe. James Bond looked at the paper as if at a poisonous snake. Then he raised
35 his eyes to those of Mr Tanaka, who was watching him with polite interest.

'It is interesting, isn't it?' said Tanaka.

'You are wrong to keep this from us,' said Bond.

'But how can we break our promise to our American friends? They have assured our government that they will pass on anything Britain needs to know.'

'Oh, no doubt Washington will pass on the message, in an altered form. I hope they already have. But you realize that it might be in their interests to keep quiet about this terrible threat that hangs over Britain? At the same time, it is in Britain's interests to use every hour in planning what to do in reply. One small step is to put into prison all Soviet citizens in Britain.'

'I understand your point of view, Mr Bond. There is, of course, in this case, another way for this information to reach your government.' Mr Tanaka gave an unpleasant smile.

'But I gave my word of honour!' said Bond.

Mr Tanaka's face changed suddenly. The dark eyes lost their glitter. He said, 'Mr Bond, I was very happy in England. Your people were very good to me. I am in great debt to your country. I have just told you a State secret. My friendship for Dikko, and your own honest and sincere manner, encouraged me. I fully realize the importance of this piece of paper to Britain. Help me to pay my debt, but you are on your honour not to tell anyone else.'

'Thank you.'

Tiger Tanaka got to his feet and held out his hand. 'Goodbye for now, Mr Bond. I hope that we shall see more of each other.' The powerful face lit up again. The great golden smile was sincere.

'A car is waiting to take you back to your hotel. Please give my best wishes to Dikko and tell him he owes me one thousand yen for repairs to a microphone, the property of the State.'

James Bond took the hard, dry hand again. He said again, from the heart, 'Thank you, Mr Tanaka.' He walked out of the little secret room with one thought in his mind. How fast could his news reach Melbourne? And from there, how fast to London?

6 The Death Collector

And now it was a month later and Mr Tanaka had become 'Tiger' and Mr Bond was 'Bondo-san.' Tiger had explained the name to Bond. 'James,' he had said, 'is a difficult word in Japanese. The hard *nd* sound, too, is difficult. When this hap-
5   pens at the end of a foreign word, we add an *o*. So you are Bondo-san. Is that all right?'
    'Does Bondo mean a pig or anything like that in Japanese?'
    'No. It has no meaning.'
    'That's fine then.'
10   The weeks had passed without any important progress in Bond's mission except in the direction of his friendship with Dikko and Tiger. Outside working hours the three men were often together, but Bond felt that Tanaka was examining him very carefully all the time. Dikko had agreed about this. 'I
15   think you're making progress, James. Something's happening in the background, but I can't tell what. I guess Tiger's asked his chief and is waiting for an answer. And if he does this favour for you, what have you got to offer in return? It ought to be something big!'
20   Bond looked doubtful. The Macao 'Blue Route' was begin-ning to look very small indeed.
    A few days later, Tiger had called Bond again to his under-ground office. Thanks to the information he had given Bond, the West had been able to act at once, and the Soviet plan
25   had failed.
    'Now, Bondo-san,' said Tiger with his wicked smile, 'you wish to use our machine. The price will be high. What can you offer in exchange?'
    'The Macao "Blue Route."' Bond described it. Tiger
30   looked sad. Deep down in the narrow eyes there was a wicked gleam. 'I am very much afraid that I have bad news for you, Bondo-san. We broke the codes almost at the begin-

ning. We already receive all the information from that route.
I can show you the papers if you wish. We have simply given
it a new name, the "Orange Route". I admit that the information is very useful. But we already have it. What other
goods can you offer in exchange?'   5

Bond had to laugh! All the work, the expense, the danger
of running the 'Blue Route' – and at least fifty percent of
that went to help Japan! I'm certainly learning something on
this trip, he thought. Just wait until I tell them in London!

'May I suggest you name a price?' said Bond. 'Or pay a   10
visit to London and inspect our goods for yourself. I am sure
my chief will be very glad to welcome you.'

For a moment Tiger Tanaka looked thoughtful. He seemed
to be turning Bond's words over in his mind. Then he closed
the meeting with the invitation to the *geisha* party, and Bond   15
went off with mixed feelings to report to Melbourne and
London.

In the room where he now sat after the *geisha* party, and
where Tiger had just cheerfully threatened him with death,
tigers' heads looked down from the walls. The chair in which   20
he sat was covered with tiger skin, and there were tiger-skin
rugs on the floor. Mr Tanaka had been born in the year of the
Tiger. Bond, Tiger was pleased to tell him, had been born in
the year of the Rat.

Bond drank some *sake.* 'My dear Tiger,' he said, 'you have   25
my word of honour.'

Tiger pulled up a chair and faced Bond across the low
table. The sound of night traffic came in from some way beyond the surrounding houses. It was the end of September,
but warm. It was ten minutes to midnight. Tiger spoke in a   30
soft voice.

'In that case, Bondo-san, I will tell you an interesting
story. For nearly a hundred years, there have been foreigners
who have come to this country and settled here. In general,
we have been kind to them, as, perhaps, the British could be   35
to a Japanese who bought a castle in Scotland and learnt the
language. Usually, such people are harmless. But one of them

is far from harmless. He entered this country in January of this year. You may laugh, Bondo-san, but this is the wickedest man I have ever known.'

'I have met many bad men in my time, Tiger, and most of
5 them have been slightly mad. Is this one mad too?'

'Oh, no. In the opinion of our highest authorities, the man is a genius. He is probably the finest collector in the world.'

'What does he collect?'

'He collects death.'

10 'You mean he kills people?' asked Bond.

'No, Bondo-san. It is not as simple as that. He persuades people to kill themselves. No, that is not exactly correct either. Let us just say that he provides an easy and attractive opportunity for people to kill themselves. So far, more than
15 five hundred Japanese have done just that.'

'Why don't you arrest him? Hang him?'

'Bondo-san, it is not as easy as that. Let me begin at the beginning. In January of this year, a gentleman called Doctor Guntram Shatterhand entered this country, quite openly.
20 With him was his wife, Frau Emmy Shatterhand. They had Swiss passports. The doctor described himself as a collector of plants, especially rare ones from hot countries. He quickly got in touch with our Ministry of Agriculture. He was ready, he told them, to spend no less than a million pounds on
25 making a garden or park of rare plants and trees from all over the world, not open to the public, but open to Japanese experts for study. A wonderful offer! Naturally, our government accepted, and in return let the good doctor stay here for ten years – a rare honour.

30   'After travelling round the country, the doctor bought an old castle in Kyushu, our southern island. The high wall around the grounds was just what the doctor wanted. An army of builders and painters moved in, and plants began arriving from all over the world. Here I must mention that a
35 second reason for the doctor's choice of that place was that it is full of volcanoes and mud-holes which provide, all the year round, the right temperature for these rare plants. The

doctor and his wife moved into the castle and began taking on staff to look after the castle and the gardens.' Tiger looked sad again. 'And at this time I realized that something was wrong. The doctor was taking on only the former members of the Black Dragon Society.'   *5*

'What's that?'

'What *was* that? The society officially broke up before the war. It was full of criminals, failed officers from the army, secret agents, also big men in industry and business, who found the Black Dragons useful to do their dirty work. And *10* the strange thing is, the doctor chose to live in just that corner of Japan that used to be the centre of the Black Dragons. There has always been a lot of crime in that district, and there still is. These societies never die out completely, and this Doctor Shatterhand found it easy to collect about *15* twenty extremely tough and dangerous men around him. He dressed them as servants and gardeners, of course.'

Tiger Tanaka paused and poured more drinks.

'Well,' asked Bond, 'have they done any harm yet?'

'Oh, no, they are only his personal servants. The trouble is *20* quite different. You see, this man Shatterhand has made a garden of death.'

Bond raised his eyebrows. Tiger gave his golden smile. 'Bondo-san, I can see from your face that you think I am either drunk or mad. Now listen. This Doctor Shatterhand *25* has filled his park with poisonous plants and trees. He has filled the lakes and streams with poisonous and man-eating fish, and he has added poisonous snakes, spiders and other creatures. He and his wife are safe from these things, because he wears a full suit of armour of the seventeenth century, and *30* she wears bee-keepers' clothing. His workers are safe because they wear high rubber boots, and masks on their faces.'

'How silly.'

Tiger handed Bond several sheets of paper. 'Be patient. Do not judge until you understand. Here is a list of these poison- *35* ous plants and trees, from our Ministry of Agriculture. Read it. You will be interested to know what charming little flowers our friend the doctor is growing.'

Bond read it. All the plants were extremely poisonous in a variety of unpleasant ways. He handed the papers back to Tiger.

5   'Don't forget the man-eating fish and the poisonous snakes Bondo-san,' said Tiger. 'Do you see what I mean now?'

'No,' said Bond, 'I don't. What exactly is the doctor trying to do?'

7　The Deadly Garden

'When you know us better, Bondo-san,' said Tiger, 'you
will know that suicide is an important, and most unfortunate,
part of the Japanese way of life.' He paused. 'Or perhaps a
most noble one. It depends on how you look at it. When you
have failed, there is no more sincere apology than offering up   5
your own life. It is all you have to give. And the more exciting the suicide is, the better — not long ago a young student became very famous by trying to cut his own head off.
Lovers hold hands and throw themselves over the very high
Kegon Falls at Nikko. The Mihara volcano is another favour-   10
ite place. But always the wheels of a good old-fashioned rail-
way train are the easiest. All you do is jump.'
　'You're a blood-thirsty thing, Tiger! But what has all this
to do with Doctor Shatterhand and his pretty garden?'
　'Everything, Bondo-san, everything. You see, much against   15
the good doctor's wishes, of course, his poison garden has become the favourite place for suicides in the whole of Japan.
It has everything: a ride on the famous express train to
Kyoto; a boat trip across our beautiful Inland Sea, so full of
Japanese history; a local train to Fukuoka and a walk or a   20
taxi ride along a beautiful coast to the beautiful Castle of
Death. Climb the walls or hide in a delivery van, and then
take a last, delicious walk through the beautiful gardens. Will
your death be easy or painful? Will a snake bite you, or will
hunger or curiosity lead you to taste one of those rich orange   25
fruit? Of course, if you want to make it quick, there is always
a mud-hole where the temperature is one thousand degrees
centigrade.
　'Official visitors must show a pass. But the suicides fight
their way in somehow. The good doctor is of course much   30
disturbed. He has put up warning notices; they act only as
advertisements. He has even gone to the expense of flying a

gas balloon from the roof of his castle. But it only says:
"Here is death — come and get it!" '

'But Tiger, why don't you arrest him and burn the place
down?'

5   'Arrest him for what? For giving Japan a wonderful collection of rare plants? Burn down a million-pound castle belong-
ing to a rich and respected foreigner? The man has done
nothing wrong. If anyone is to blame, it is the Japanese
people. But it is certainly strange that, when the ambulance

10   comes, the victims are always very dead indeed, usually in the
form of a bag of bones from the red-hot mud-holes. The Doctor, too, is puzzled. He suggests that the victims fall into the
mud-holes by mistake, after the poisonous plants have blinded
them or sent them mad. Maybe. But his score so far is over

15   five hundred. We must put a stop to it.'

'What have you done so far?'

'Officials have visited the doctor. He was most polite. He
asked them to protect him from these unwanted visitors.
They interfere with his work, he says, and pick valuable

20   plants. The doctor says he will do anything in his power to
help, except leave his garden, which he loves so much and
which is of so much interest to scientists. He has made another very generous offer. He is starting a special department
— which workers of his own choice will run, of course — to

25   take the poisons from his trees and plants and give them free
to Japanese hospitals. You will know, of course, that many
of these poisons, in a weak form, are valuable medicines.'

'But how does all this affect you?' Bond was now getting
sleepy. It was four o'clock and the sky was lighter above the

30   grey line of roofs. He drank down the last of the *sake*. It was
time for bed. But Tiger did not seem to worry about the late-
ness of the hour. His face was hard and angry as he said, 'One
month ago, Bondo-san, under orders from my chiefs, I sent
one of my best men into this place. He had to discover what

35   it was all about. One week later, Bondo-san, we pulled him
out of the water near the Castle of Death. He was blind and
mad. All the lower half of his body was terribly burned. All

he could say before his death, which came soon, was "Pink dragon-flies above the graves".'

James Bond felt that he was living inside a dream. Why was Tiger telling him this? Because he was lonely? Because there was no one else he could trust? 'What did you do next, Tiger?'   5
asked Bond.

Tiger Tanaka looked very directly at James Bond and said, 'What was there to do? I did nothing except apologize to my chiefs. I waited for the right person to come along. I waited for *you*.'   10

'Me!'

Tiger said, and it was an order, 'Bondo-san, if you have any love for your country, you leave tomorrow.' He looked at his watch. 'By the twelve-twenty from Tokyo main station. You will not go back to your hotel, or see Dikko. From now on,   15
you are under my personal orders.' The voice was very quiet and smooth. 'Do you understand?'

'What in God's name are you talking about?' asked Bond.

'In my office the other day, you told me to name my price for the code-breaking machine. This is it.'   20

'But what?'

'You must enter the Castle of Death and kill the Dragon within.'

8   Instant Japan

And now the big car was flying through the empty streets towards a bath-house which, Tiger said, was very special and very pleasant indeed.

Tiger had overcome all Bond's objections. On all the evidence, this doctor had planted a garden of death. Because he was mad? Because it amused him? Tiger did not know, and he did not care. He had decided that a foreigner must carry out this mission, and Bond seemed the ideal man for the job. He had had a lot of practice in such secret operations and, if the Japanese police arrested him, he and Tiger could tell a story about the British secret service. If he failed in his mission, then the doctor and his guards could kill him – too bad.

'But,' argued Bond, 'I've got nothing against this man. He's never done anything to me.'

'Bondo-san, this man has already killed five hundred people. He deserves to die. And, in any case, we are employing you to do this job for us in exchange for our code-breaking machine. Surely that makes you feel better?'

Bond had agreed. 'But it's an impossible mission,' he had said. 'For a foreigner, anyway. They'll see me miles away!'

'Not after I've finished with you,' said Tiger, with his wicked smile. So now, at this quiet little bath-house, Bond was going to receive his new Japanese personality.

'Here,' Tiger told him, 'you will receive your first treatment and then get some sleep. Then we shall take the train together.'

They arrived at a wide-open doorway with a view of polished floors behind, and three bowing, smiling women in Japanese dress. They were as bright as birds although it was nearly five in the morning. After much bowing, Bond took off his shoes and followed one of the women along a passage and through an open partition into a bathroom. Bond turned

to the older woman, who was just closing the partition, and
said, 'Tanaka-san' in a desperate voice.

Tiger came. 'What is it now?' he said. 'Really, you must
learn to obey orders without asking questions, Bondo-san.
You see that box? The girl will put you in the box, which has   *5*
a fire under it. You will sweat. After perhaps ten minutes she
will help you out of the box and she will wash you. She will
then pour a very strong dark dye into that bath in the floor,
and you will get in. You will wash your face and hair. She
will then cut your hair in the Japanese style. You will then go   *10*
to sleep. She will wake you with eggs and coffee, you will
shave, and that will be the end.

'And now, please do not disturb me any more. I am going
to enjoy myself in a similar manner, but without the dark
dye. And please, in future, have faith. You are going to have   *15*
some new experiences. Enjoy them. All right? Then goodnight, my dear Bondo-san. The night will be short, and,' Tiger
gave his golden smile again, 'at the end of it you will be a new
man.' Later, sweating in the wooden box, Bond decided to
take Tiger's advice.   *20*

It was indeed a new man who followed Tiger through the
crowded halls of Tokyo main station. Bond's face and hands
were a light brown. His black hair, oiled until it shone, was
cut in the Japanese style, and his eyebrows were shaved to
look Japanese. He was dressed, like so many of the other   *25*
travellers, in a white cotton shirt and a cheap black tie. He
wore black trousers with a cheap plastic belt, and black plastic
shoes and dark blue socks. He carried an old Japan Air Lines
bag over his shoulder. This contained a change of clothes and
some Japanese cigarettes. In his pockets were a comb, a   *30*
cheap, used wallet containing about five thousand yen in
notes, and a strong pocket knife.

In spite of his height, James Bond was now one of the
crowd, and nobody even glanced at him.

'We will move your clothes from the hotel to Dikko's   *35*
apartment,' Tiger had said. 'Later today, Dikko will inform
your chief that you have left Tokyo with me and that you

will be away for several days. Dikko believes this. My own
department knows only that I shall be absent on a mission to
Fukuoka. They do not know that you are with me. And now
we are on our way to the fishing port of Toba. There we will
5 spend the night. This will be a slow journey so that I can
train and educate you. I must make you familiar with Japanese customs so that you make as few mistakes as possible
when the time comes.'

The shining orange and silver express train slid to a stop
10 beside them. Tiger pushed his way on. Bond waited politely
for two or three women to go before him. When he sat down
beside Tiger, Tiger whispered angrily, 'First lesson, Bondo-
san! Do not make way for women! Push them, walk over
them. You may be polite to very old men, but to no one else.
15 Is that clear?'

'Tiger, you're a hard master.'

'I certainly am. But now let us go and get something to eat
and drink in the restaurant-car.'

James Bond tried hard with his chopsticks and slices of
20 raw fish on a pile of rice. 'You must get accustomed to Japanese food, Bondo-san,' Tiger said. Bond watched the coast-
line out of the window and he was lost in thought when he
felt a hard push from behind. He turned and saw the square
back of a man, moving into the next carriage. When they
25 went back to their seats, Bond found that his wallet was gone.
Tiger was surprised. 'That is very unusual in Japan,' he said.
'But it doesn't matter. I will get you another at Toba. I will
not call the guard. We do not wish to draw attention to ourselves. And there is no way of finding the thief. I regret this,
30 Bondo-san. I hope you will forget it.'

'Of course. It's nothing.'

They left the train at Gamagori, a pretty sea-side village,
and the short boat trip that followed was most pleasant. As
they got out, Bond saw a square back in the crowd, like the
35 man in the restaurant-car. But he dismissed the thought and
followed Tiger along the narrow streets.

'We shall go to a restaurant,' said Tiger. 'I have ordered

sake in large quantities, and then. a special dinner of lobster.'

Bond felt a little happier. They reached the restaurant. The *sake* came, and the girl who served it was pretty. Tiger had ordered large glasses. Bond swallowed his very fast.

'Your disgusting drinking habits will suit the part you will play, Bondo-san.'

'And what will that be?'

'A coal-miner from Fukuoka. There are many tall men in that job. We shall fill your finger-nails with coal dust when the time comes. You are deaf and dumb. Here is your card. If someone talks to you, show that and they will stop. They may also give you a few small coins. Accept them and bow.'

'Thanks *very* much!'

'And now, Bondo-san, it is my duty to entertain a friend as well as to instruct a pupil. Here comes the lobster.'

Rice, raw eggs and bowls of sliced seaweed appeared in front of both of them. Then each received a fine dish with a large lobster in it. The head and tail were still on, with the flesh sliced and pink in the centre. Bond picked up his chopsticks. He was surprised to find that the flesh was raw. He was even more surprised when the head of his lobster began moving off his dish.

'Tiger!' Bond said in horror. 'The thing's alive!'

Tiger whispered impatiently, 'Really, Bondo-san, I am most disappointed in you. I sincerely hope you will improve during our journey. Now eat up! This is a very great Japanese dish.'

James Bond bowed low.

'You will soon become accustomed to the Japanese way of life,' said Tiger gracefully.

'It's their way of death that puzzles me,' said Bond, and he handed his glass to the kneeling girl for more *sake* to give him strength to try the seaweed.

9 Advanced Studies

Tiger and Bond stood under the trees and observed the people who were visiting the Temple of Ise.

'All right,' said Tiger, 'you have observed these people and their actions. They have been saying prayers to the sun-
5 goddess. Go and say a prayer without drawing attention to yourself.'

Bond walked through the great wooden arch and joined the crowd. Two priests were watching. Bond bowed, threw a coin into the bowl, clapped his hands loudly, bent his head in
10 prayer, clapped his hands again, bowed and walked out.

'You did well,' said Tiger. 'One of the priests looked at you; the public paid no attention. Next time, clap your hands more loudly. Then the goddess will pay more attention to your prayer. Now we will go back to the car and continue
15 our journey.'

In the parking place crowds of students were climbing in and out of buses. Tiger led the way through the middle of the crowd. When they reached the car, Tiger looked pleased. 'Did you notice anything, Bondo-san?'
20 'Only a lot of pretty girls.'

'Wrong. Nobody recognized you as a foreigner. Your appearance is one thing, but your behaviour has also improved. You are more at home.' Tiger gave his great golden smile. 'The Tanaka system is not so foolish as you think.
25 'Now, Bondo-san,' said Tiger, 'I am taking you to one of our secret training schools. It is not far from here, in a castle in the mountains. It is here that my agents learn *ninjutsu*, which means the art of the spy. You will see men walk across the surface of water, walk up walls and across ceilings,
30 and you will see equipment which makes it possible for them to stay under water for a full day. And many other tricks too. I think you will be interested and perhaps learn some-

thing yourself. I have never approved of agents carrying guns and other weapons. In China, Korea and East Russia, where my agents work, to have a weapon at all is a confession of guilt. My men must be able to kill without weapons. All they may carry is a stick and a length of thin chain. You under- *5* stand?'

'Yes, that makes sense. We have a similar training school too.'

Back on the open, dusty road, something made Bond look through the rear window of the car. Far behind, there was a *10* man on a motor-cycle. Later, when they turned up a minor road into the mountains, he was still there. Bond told Tiger, but Tiger dismissed the matter.

The castle stood on a mountain. There was water around it. Tiger showed his pass at the entrance. As the car came to a *15* stop, young men in shorts and running shoes came out of the castle and stood behind three older men. They bowed almost to the ground as Tiger climbed out of the car. Tiger and Bond bowed too. Tiger then spoke fast Japanese to the middle-aged man who was clearly in charge of the team. This man turned *20* to the students, whose ages seemed to be between twenty-five and thirty-five. He called numbers and six men ran off into the castle. Tiger commented to Bond, 'They will put on special clothes and go and look for the man who was follow-ing you. If anyone is in the grounds, they will bring him to *25* us. And now we will see a little attack on the castle.' Tiger shouted more orders, and the other men ran off. Perhaps a quarter of an hour later, there came a whistle from the walls above them and at once ten men came out of the forest on their left. They were dressed from head to foot in black, and *30* only their eyes showed through holes in the black masks. They ran to the edge of the moat, put on strips of light wood, and slid across the water on these, until they reached the bottom of the giant black wall. There they took off their strips of wood, took lengths of rope and a handful of small *35* iron climbing-nails out of their pockets, and almost ran up the walls like fast black spiders.

Tiger turned to Bond. 'You understand that it is night-time. In a few days, you will have to do something similar. Note that the ropes end in an iron hook which they throw up and catch between the stones of the wall.' The instructor said something to Tiger and pointed. Tiger nodded. He said to 5 Bond, 'The man at the end is the weakest of the team. The instructor thinks he will soon fall.'

The line of climbing men was now almost at the top of the two-hundred-foot wall, and, sure enough, with only a few feet to go, the end man fell with a scream of fear. His body 10 hit the wall once, then crashed down into the water. The instructor took off his shirt and dived the hundred feet down into the water. He swam quickly towards the body that lay face downwards. Tiger turned to Bond.

'It is not important. He was going to fail the man anyway. 15 And now come into the courtyard, and see some fighting with sticks.'

Bond took a last glance at the instructor, who was now dragging the body to the shore. Bond wondered if any of the students was going to fail his stick-fighting test. Failure was 20 certainly total here!

In the courtyard, pairs of men were fighting with thick sticks about two yards long. At last there was a loud whistle, and it was over. A doctor appeared and looked after the injured men, and those who were still on their feet bowed to 25 each other, to Bond and to Tiger. Tiger spoke fiercely to them in Japanese. 'I'm telling them how well they did,' he whispered to Bond. Then he led Bond into the castle to drink tea and see the *ninja* weapons. These included steel wheels the size of a large coin, to spin on a finger and throw. There 30 were chains with weights at each end.

'We use these as the cowboys in South America do, only we catch men instead of cattle,' Tiger told Bond.

There were sharp nails twisted into knots, to damage the bare feet of whoever was following. Bond remembered similar 35 things which the French used during the war against the tyres of the enemy cars. There were hollow lengths of bamboo for

breathing under water (Bond had used the same trick once in the West Indies). There were various brass gloves for fighting with the fists. There were also gloves with their palms covered with very sharp little hooks, for 'walking' up walls, and many
5 more similar weapons. Bond made polite noises of amazement. Out in the courtyard again, the leader of the special group reported motor-cycle tracks that stopped and turned back a mile from the castle. That was the only sign of anyone following. Then came the bows and the goodbyes, and they
10 were on their way again, to Kyoto this time.

'Well, Bondo-san. What do you think of my training-school?'

'I can imagine that the skills the students learn there are most valuable, but I wonder what happens if you get caught
15 with your black suit and your mask and all your *ninja* weapons? But they certainly went up that wall fast, and that stick-fighting must be very effective against a criminal with a bicycle chain or a knife. I must get a six-foot walking-stick for myself!'

20 Tiger looked impatient. 'You speak like a man who only knows the sort of fighting that goes on in a cheap Western film. *That* will be no use to you in spying in North Korea, dressed as a simple countryman with his stick.'

James Bond was tired out. He was also feeling sorry for the
25 student who had died. He made no reply.

10 You Only Live Twice

To Bond's great relief they stayed that night at the best hotel in Kyoto, which had comfortable beds. Better still, Tiger had to dine with the Chief of Police and Bond had supper and drinks in his room. Then he watched Japanese television for a while, went to bed and slept for twelve hours. 5

The next morning they drove to Osaka for their boat-trip across the Inland Sea to the southern island of Kyushu. The ship was very modern and comfortable, and Tiger and Bond sat in the first-class dining room and enjoyed lunch. Tiger was determined to increase Bond's knowledge of Japanese life. 10 'Bondo-san, I wonder if I can ever make you understand Japanese poetry. Have you ever heard of Bashō, for example?'

'No,' said Bond with polite interest. 'Who's he?'

'Just so,' said Tiger. 'And yet I have heard of Shakespeare, Homer, Dante, Cervantes and Goethe. And yet Bashō, who is 15 the equal of any of them, is unknown to you.'

'What did he write?'

'He was particularly fond of the *haiku*, the verse of seventeen syllables.' Tiger said, in a thoughtful voice,

' "The butterfly is perfuming 20
    its wings, in the scent
    of the flower." '

He looked at Bond hopefully.

'Doesn't mean much to me,' said Bond.

'You do not appreciate the quality of these verses? Well, 25 do me a favour, Bondo-san. Write a *haiku* for me yourself. I am sure you can if you try. After all, you must have had *some* education?'

Bond laughed. 'Mostly in Latin and Greek — absolutely no help in ordering a cup of coffee in Rome or Athens after- 30 wards! But give me a pen and some paper and I'll have a try.'

Tiger gave him the pen and paper. Bond put his head in his

hands. Finally, after much crossing out and re-writing, he
said, 'Tiger, how's this?' He read out:
'   "You only live twice:
         Once when you are born
5   And once when you look death in the face." '
Tiger clapped his hands softly. He said with real delight,
'But that is excellent, Bondo-san. Most sincere.' He took the
pen and paper again and wrote something in Japanese. He
shook his head. 'No, it won't go into Japanese. You have the
10 wrong number of syllables. But it is a most honourable attempt.' He looked at Bond. 'You were perhaps thinking of
your mission?'
      'Perhaps.'
      'Is it worrying you?'
15   'The practical difficulties, yes.'
      'Then you are not concerned with your own safety?'
      'Not particularly. I've had worse jobs before.'
      'You have courage. You do not appear to value your life as
highly as most Western men.' Tiger looked at him kindly. 'Is
20 there perhaps a reason for that?'
      'Not that I can think of. Now, Tiger, stop trying to read
my mind! More *sake*!'
      Tiger ordered the *sake*. They arrived at Beppu in the
southern island of Kyushu as the sun was setting. 'Just the
25 time,' said Tiger, 'to see the famous red-hot mud-springs here.
There will be no time in the morning as we shall have to start
early for Fukuoka.'
      Bond's heart sank. Soon, he thought, the sight-seeing and
the *sake* will have to stop!
30   Above the town of Beppu, they visited each of the ten hot
springs. The hot mud was in different colours — red, blue and
orange — and everywhere there were warning notices to keep
visitors at a safe distance. Beside one was a notice in English
and Japanese: 'This volcano erupts every twenty minutes.'
35 They joined a small crowd and waited. In five minutes there
came a noise from underground and hot grey mud shot into
the air and splashed down again. As Bond was turning away,

he noticed a large red wheel. There were warning notices beside it. Bond asked Tiger about it.

'It says that this wheel controls the volcano, lets the mud erupt. If it is screwed down, pressure will build up inside and the whole place will blow up. It is, of course, all nonsense to attract the tourists. But now, back to the town, Bondo-san! Since it is our last day together – on this mission, that is – I have arranged a special feast. I ordered it by radio from the ship. A *fugu* feast!'

Bond cursed silently. What new horror was this?

'*Fugu* is a Japanese fish. Its flesh is particularly delicious. The fish is also very popular with suicides and murderers because certain parts of it contain a poison which brings instant death.'

'How very thoughtful of you, Tiger!'

They left their bags at a Japanese hotel where Tiger had reserved rooms. They enjoyed a bath together and then went off for their dinner. Bond enjoyed Japanese bathing habits. Was it because they washed *outside* the bath that the Japanese smelt so clean?

The restaurant had a giant *fugu* fish hanging as a sign above the door, and inside, to Bond's relief, there were Western chairs and tables. Their table was ready. Bond said, 'Now then, Tiger, I'm not going to attempt honourable suicide without at least five jugs of *sake* inside me.' The *sake* came, and Bond swallowed it all.

'Now bring on this poison fish,' he said fiercely, 'and if it kills me it will be doing the good Doctor a favour!'

Pretty girls brought a beautiful white dish as big as a bicycle wheel. On it, arranged like a huge flower, were slices of raw white fish. Bond started on it with his chopsticks. He was becoming quite skilful with these.

The fish tasted of nothing, not even fish. But it was very pleasant and Bond, seeing Tiger enjoying it, praised it highly. There followed various side-dishes and more *sake*.

Bond sat back and lit a cigarette. He said, 'Well, Tiger, this is nearly the end of my education. Tomorrow, as you say, I

must leave school and go out into the world. How many
marks out of a hundred?'

'You have done well, Bondo-san, apart from making
Western jokes about Eastern customs. And your company has
5   given me much pleasure and a certain amount of amusement.
I will give you seventy-five marks out of a hundred.'

As they rose to go, a man pushed past Bond to get to the
exit. Bond knew him. It was the man on the train!

Well, well, thought Bond. If he shows up on the way to
10   Fukuoka, I'll get him! But it looks like nothing out of hundred to Tiger for observation.

11   A Date with Death

At six in the morning a car from the Chief of Police in Fukuoka came for them. There were two policemen in the front
seat. They drove off along the coast. After a while, Bond
said, 'Tiger, somebody is following us. I don't care what you
say. The man who stole my wallet was in the *fugu* restaurant   5
last night, and now he's a mile behind on a motor-cycle.
Please tell the driver to go up a side-road and then go after
him and get him. I'm usually right about these things. Please
do as I say.'

Tiger looked back and then gave instructions to the driver.   10
The driver nodded and the policeman at his side took out his
gun. They came to a rough track on the left. The driver
turned in out of sight of the road and stopped his engine.
They listened, and soon the noise of a motor-cycle passed the
end of the track. The driver drove off after him. Tiger gave   15
more sharp instructions. He said to Bond, 'I have told him to
try warning the man with his siren and, if he doesn't stop, to
ride him into the ditch.'

'Well, I'm glad you're giving him a chance,' said Bond. 'I
may be wrong and he may only be somebody in a hurry.'   20

They soon caught up with the man. The driver said something. Tiger translated, 'He says it's a powerful, fast motor-
cycle. He can easily get away from us on it. But even Japanese criminals are men of discipline. He will prefer to obey
the siren.'   25

The siren screamed. The man glanced over his shoulder. He
came slowly to a stop. His right hand went inside his jacket.
Bond had his hand on the door-handle. He said, 'Watch out,
Tiger! He's got a gun!' As they pulled up alongside, Bond
threw himself out of the door and crashed into the man,   30
knocking him and his machine to the ground. The policeman
beside the driver took a flying leap and the two bodies rolled

into the ditch. Almost immediately the policeman got to his feet. The man was dead.

Tiger walked down into the ditch. He pulled up the man's right sleeve. There was a small black Japanese sign on his arm.

5 'You were right, Bondo-san,' said Tiger. 'He is a Black Dragon.'

The two policemen were standing looking politely puzzled. Tiger gave them orders. They searched the man's clothes and took out various objects, including Bond's wallet, with the

10 five thousand yen still in it, and a cheap diary. They handed everything to Tiger, then dragged the body out of the ditch and pushed it roughly into the boot of the car. Then they hid the motor-cycle in some bushes and got back into the car.

After a few moments Tiger said thoughtfully, 'I can't be-

15 lieve it! These people know all my movements. Everything we have done in the past week, and all our stopping-places on our journey, are in this diary. He simply describes you as a foreigner. But perhaps he has telephoned a description. I have been careless, Bondo-san. I apologize. But at least you have

20 seen an example of Doctor Shatterhand's methods. There is certainly more to this than there seems to be. At some time in his life, this man has been a spy, I am sure of that. He has discovered who I am — and that is a State secret. He has recognized me as his chief enemy. He is either a great mad-

25 man or a great criminal. You agree, Bondo-san?'

'You're probably right. I can hardly wait to *see* him!'

The local police station was just off the main street of Fu-kuoka. The Chief of Police received them politely. A giant photograph of the Castle of Death, taken from the air, was

30 on the desk. Tiger said, 'Please examine this photograph, Bondo-san.'

Bond looked, and decided he couldn't do it. The castle grounds covered the whole of a small piece of land that stuck out to sea. The two-hundred foot cliff was strengthened with

35 giant stone blocks, down to the breaking waves, to form a huge wall that sloped slightly up to the guns and the watch-towers. From the top of this wall there seemed to be a ten-

foot drop into the park. There were many trees and bushes
between winding streams. There was a broad lake with an
island in its centre. Steam seemed to rise from the lake and
there were occasional signs of it among the trees too. At the
back of the park stood the castle. It was protected from the 5
countryside around it by a fairly low wall.

'Bondo-san,' said Tiger, 'it is over this wall that the suicides
get in. The Chief of Police says that a secret approach from
that side is now very difficult. The suicides pay local people
to lead them here,' – and he pointed – 'and there are places 10
in the walls which are constantly changed and kept open for
the suicides. Every time the Chief of Police puts a guard at
one of them, another one is made known to the local people
by the castle guards. The Chief of Police says he is thinking
of resigning.' 15

'Of course,' said Bond, 'and then suicide by *fugu* poison-
ing, perhaps.' He turned back to the photograph. The castle
itself was a giant Japanese-style building with decorated roofs
like a castle in a fairy-story. Bond looked carefully at the picture, but there was nothing more to learn from it. 'However 20
can I get in there without being seen?' he asked.

'The Chief of Police says that if you are a good swimmer,
there is a chance. I have sent for a complete set of *ninja*
equipment for you from my training school. The sea wall
will present no problems.' 25

'I can swim well enough, but how do I get to the base of
the sea wall? Where do I start from?'

'The Chief of Police says there is an Ama island called
Kuro only half a mile out to sea.'

'What's an Ama island?' 30

'The Ama are a people whose girls dive for shells and
pearls. Some of them are very beautiful. But the Ama do not
encourage visitors to their islands. They have their own customs.'

'Sounds interesting, but how am I going to stay on this 35
Kuro island? I may have to wait days for the weather to be
right.'

'The Chief of Police knows a family on Kuro. It is a most interesting family. There is a father and a mother and one daughter. Her name is Kissy Suzuki. I have heard of her. When she was seventeen, she was chosen to go to Hollywood
5   to make a film. They wanted a Japanese diving girl of great beauty, and someone had heard of her. She made the film, but hated Hollywood and wanted only to return to her island, so she came home. She was quite famous at the time, but Kissy is now twenty-three and everyone has forgotten
10   about her. The Chief of Police says that he could arrange for you to stay with this family. He says that it is a simple house, but comfortable because of the money that Kissy earned in Hollywood. The other houses on the island are nothing but fishermen's huts.'

15   'But will the others let me stay?'

'The Chief of Police will speak to the priest. There will be no trouble.'

'All right,' said Bond, 'so I stay on this island, and then one night I swim across to the wall. How do I get up it?'

20   'You will have the *ninja* equipment. You will use it. It is very simple.'

'As I saw, from the man who fell into the water! Then what do I do?'

'You hide in the grounds and wait for an opportunity to
25   kill him. How you do that is up to you. As I told you, he goes about in armour. A man in armour is easy to kill. You only need to knock him off his feet. Then you will kill him with your *ninja* chain. If his wife is with him, you will kill her also. Then you will escape over the wall and swim back to
30   Kuro. A police boat will come and pick you up.'

Bond said doubtfully, 'Well, it all sounds very simple. But what about the guards? The place is full of them.'

'You must just keep out of their way. As you can see, the park is full of hiding-places.'

35   'Thanks very much. In one of those poison-bushes or up a poison-tree. I don't want to be blind, or mad.'

'The *ninja* clothing will give you complete protection. You

will also wear a swimmer's mask to protect your eyes. You
will pull all this equipment behind you in a plastic bag.'
  'My dear Tiger, you've thought of everything. But why
can't I have just one little gun?'
  'Bondo-san, you must kill silently. *Ninjutsu* is the only   5
way.'
  'Oh, all right,' said Bond. 'Now, has the Chief of Police got
a photograph of this man?'
  The photograph had been taken from a long way away
with a special camera. It showed a giant figure in ancient   10
Japanese chain armour. Bond studied the photograph carefully, noting the weak spots at the neck and the joints. He wore
a metal shield, and a wide Japanese sword hung from his
waist. There was no sign of any other weapon. Bond said
thoughtfully, 'He doesn't look as silly as he ought to. Prob-   15
ably because of that castle in the background. Have you got a
picture of his face? Perhaps he looks madder without his
armour!'
  The Chief of Police gave Bond a passport photograph.
Bond looked at it, and felt himself become stiff all over. He   20
said to himself, 'My God!' Yes, there was no doubt. The man
had grown a black beard, but there could be no doubt. Bond
looked up. He said, 'Have you got one of the woman?'
  The Chief of Police saw the look of controlled hate on
Bond's face. He bowed, and produced another picture. Yes,   25
there she was, the ugly beast! The flat, cruel face, the dull
eyes, the thin ugly hair. Bond held the pictures, not looking
at them.
  So here they were! The people who had murdered Bond's
wife! Ernst Stavro Blofeld and Irma Bunt. They of all people! 30
Could they smell him coming? Had the dead spy discovered
his name and told them? Did they know that an enemy was
on his way? Bond looked up from the pictures. He was in
control of himself now. This was a private matter. It had
nothing to do with Tiger or Japan. It had nothing to do with   35
the code machine. It was a personal battle.
  James Bond decided to keep the knowledge to himself. He

did not want others to know who Doctor Shatterhand and
his wife really were. *That* would bring the Japanese and
American Secret Services down to Fukuoka to arrest Blofeld
and Irma Bunt. Bond did not want that. What he wanted was
5   revenge, personal revenge.

12 Kissy Suzuki

James Bond went through the rest of the morning in a dream. While he tried on his *ninja* equipment and watched each piece being carefully packed into a floating plastic container, his mind was full of his enemy — this man Blofeld, the great criminal, the man who was wanted by the police of the whole 5 western world. The man who had murdered Bond's wife only nine months before. And, in those nine months, this evil genius had invented a new method of collecting death. The personality of Doctor Shatterhand, the rich lover of rare plants, must be one of the many that he had wisely built up 10 over the years. Easy! A few gifts of rare plants to famous gardens, and all the time in the back of his mind the plan to retire one day and start his own garden. And what a garden! A trap for human beings who wanted to die. And of course Japan, with the worst suicide figures in the world, a country 15 with a thirst for everything that was strange, cruel or terrible, provided the perfect place. Blofeld must be mad, Bond decided, but with the madness of a genius, which he certainly was. The whole idea was on Blofeld's usual grand scale. And now the two enemies were facing each other again, but this 20 time Bond wished to kill his enemy not from duty, but for revenge! And with what weapons? Nothing but his bare hands, a small knife and a thin chain of steel. Well, he had used similar weapons before. Surprise was the best weapon of all. 25

They drove to where the police boat was waiting. They set off across the beautiful bay into the Sea of Genkai. Tiger produced sandwiches and drinks for each of them, and they ate their lunch as the green coast with its sandy beaches passed by. Tiger pointed out a dot in the distance. 'Kuro 30 Island,' he said. 'Think of all those beautiful girls, Bondo-san!'

'And the sharks who will already be gathering at the news of my swim to the castle!'

'If they do not eat the Amas, why will they eat a tough Englishman? Look at those two eagles in the sky! That is a sign of good luck.'

The small dot in the distance grew larger and soon they could see an island with cliffs and a small harbour facing north. On the mainland, Doctor Shatterhand's land reached out into the sea, and the great black walls stood high above the waves. Above them were the tops of trees, and behind them, in the distance, the roof of the castle. Bond thought of the night-swim across the bay, and the climb up those high walls. Ah well! He turned his attention back to Kuro Island.

He saw a little village and out at sea were about thirty rowing-boats. Naked children were playing among the big smooth rocks, and there were green nets hung up to dry. It was a pretty scene, like small fishing villages all over the world. Bond liked it at once. He felt that this place was waiting for him, friendly and welcoming.

The old men of the village, with the serious expressions of simple people on important occasions, came down to the boat to welcome them. The priest led them, a man of simple dignity with a round face and a sharp eye. They continued up the path of the main street to the priest's house. They entered and sat on the polished wood floor in front of the priest. The Chief of Police made a long speech. The priest made a short speech in return, to which the Chief of Police and Tiger listened politely. Tiger replied, and the business was over except for the tea.

'What did you say, Tiger?' asked Bond.

'No use telling lies to the priest. He is no fool. We told him most of the truth. He says he is sorry that you must take a human life, but he agrees that the castle is a most evil place. He will allow you to stay on the island for as long as necessary.'

'Please thank him for me,' said Bond.

'The priest will ask the Suzuki family to make you welcome. He will tell the others that you are a famous foreign expert, here to study the Ama way of life. You must therefore study it, but please behave in a sincere manner.' Here Tiger gave his wicked smile, 'Which means, do not interfere with the girls!'   5

In the evening they walked back to where the boat was tied up. The sea was dark blue and calm as a mirror. The little boats were coming back. The entire population of Kuro, perhaps two hundred, was waiting to greet the girl divers. The older people held blankets to warm the girls on their way   10 home to their hot baths. It was now five o'clock.

'They will be asleep by eight,' said Tiger, 'and out again with the dawn. You will have to change your habits, Bondo-san. The Ama live very simply, very cheaply . . . And please be polite to Kissy's parents, especially her father.'   15

Eager hands pulled each boat up onto the beach. To Bond, the girls all seemed beautiful and gay in the soft evening light. One girl, rather taller than the others, seemed to pay no attention to the strangers or to the police boat. She was the centre of a crowd of laughing girls as she walked over the shining   20 black stones and up the beach. Then an old woman held out a rough brown blanket and wrapped her in it. The couple, the old woman and the young one, walked up the beach. The young one talked excitedly. The old one listened and nodded. The priest was waiting for them. They bowed very low. He   25 talked to them and they listened, glancing occasionally at the men down below. The tall girl pulled her blanket more closely round her, James Bond had guessed it already. Now he knew. This was Kissy Suzuki.

The three people, the priest, the brown-faced old woman,   30 and the tall naked girl wrapped in her blanket, walked towards the police boat. The women stopped and the priest came forward. He bowed to Bond and spoke to him. Tiger translated: 'He says that the father and mother of Kissy Suzuki will be happy to receive you in their home. They   35 regret that they are not accustomed to Western ways, but their daughter speaks English because of her work in America

and will do her best to help. The priest asks if you can row a
boat. The father, who used to row for his daughter, is old and
stiff now. Can you take his place?'

Bond bowed. 'Please tell the priest that I shall be proud to
5 be a guest under the roof of Suzuki-san. My needs are simple
and few and I enjoy the Japanese way of life very much. I
shall be most pleased to row the family boat or help in any
other way.' He added quietly to Tiger, 'Tiger, I may need
these people's help when the time comes. Particularly the
10 girl's. How much can I tell her?'

Tiger said softly, 'Do as you think best. The priest knows,
therefore the girl can know. She can keep a secret. And now
come forward and let the priest introduce you. Don't forget
that your name here is Taro, which means "first son", Todo-
15 roki, which means "thunder". The priest is not interested in
your real name. Nobody will care. But you must try to put
on a Japanese personality for the time when you get to the
other side. The name is on your "deaf and dumb" card, and
on your miner's card too. You need not bother with these
20 things here. You are among friends. But, on the other side, if
they catch you, you will show them your "deaf and dumb"
card. All right?'

Tiger spoke to the priest, then led Bond forward to the
two women. He bowed to the mother, but remembered not
25 to bow too low ('She is only a woman,' Tiger had warned
him), and then he turned to the girl.

She laughed gaily. She said, 'You don't have to bow to me
and I shall never bow to you.' She held out her hand. 'How
do you do? My name is Kissy Suzuki.'

30 The hand was ice-cold. Bond said, 'My name is Taro Todoroki and I am sorry to keep you here so long. You are cold
and you must go and have your hot bath. It is very kind of
your family to accept me. Are you sure it's all right?'

'Whatever the priest says is all right. And I have been cold
35 before. When you have finished with your friends, my
mother and I will take you to our house. I hope you are good
at washing vegetables.'

Bond was delighted. He said, 'I studied it at college! What time do we take out the boat tomorrow?'

'About five-thirty. When the sun comes up. Perhaps you will bring me good luck. The shells are not easy to find. We had a lucky day today, but it is not always like that. Now say   *5* goodbye to your friends.'

Goodbyes were short. It was getting dark. Bond thanked the Chief of Police, who wished him luck. Tiger looked serious. He took Bond's hand in both of his, an unusual thing for a Japanese to do. He said, 'Bondo-san, I am certain you   *10* will succeed, so I will not wish you luck. But I want to give you this little present in case, through no fault of yours, things go wrong, very wrong.' He took out a little box and gave it to Bond.

Bond opened it. Inside was one long brown poison pill.   *15* Bond gave it back to Tiger. 'No thanks, Tiger. As Bashō said, or almost said, "You only live twice". And if my second life comes up, I prefer to look it in the face. But thank you, for this and for everything. Those live lobsters were really delicious. I shall now look forward to eating lots of seaweed   *20* while I'm here . . . See you in about a week.'

Tiger got down into the boat. The engine started and soon the boat was round the sea-wall and out of sight. Bond turned away. The priest had gone. Kissy Suzuki said impatiently, 'Come along, Todoroki-san. The priest says I must treat you   *25* as an equal. But give me one of your bags to carry. The village people will be watching, so let's wear the Eastern face in public.'

And the tall man with the dark face and short black hair, and the tall girl, and the old woman, walked away together   *30* along the shore.

13 One Golden Day

Dawn came in a beautiful mist of gold and blue. Bond went
outside and ate his vegetables and rice, and drank his tea, sitting on the clean white door-step of the little house. Indoors,
the women talked like happy birds as they did their house-
5 work.

They had given Bond the room of honour, the small sitting-
room with its mats, small pieces of furniture and a bird in a
cage 'in case you get lonely,' as Kissy had explained. Here
they had spread his bed on the ground and he had, for the
10 first time, and with some success, tried sleeping with his head
on a Japanese wooden pillow. The evening before, the father,
a grey old man with stiff legs and bright, bird-like eyes, had
laughed with and at him as Kissy translated Bond's story of
some of his adventures with Tiger. From the first, nobody
15 was nervous. The priest had said that Bond must be treated as
a member of the family and, although his appearance and
some of his manners were strange, Kissy apparently approved
of him, and the parents followed her. Later, after the soft
movements in the other two rooms had stopped, Bond had
20 slept happily.

Now Kissy came out of the house. She was wearing a white
cotton dress and a white cotton scarf around her thick, black
hair. She wore her equipment, the weights and the heavy flat
pick over her dress, and only her arms and her feet were bare.
25 She said, 'This is a special dress for diving in the presence of
important visitors. The priest instructed me to wear it when I
dive with you, as a mark of respect.'

'Well, let's go. We'll beat the record today. How many
shells shall we hope for?'
30 'Fifty is good. A hundred is wonderful. But above all,
you must row well and not let me drown. And you must be
kind to David.'

'Who's David?' asked Bond. He suddenly felt jealous at the thought of not having this girl to himself.

'Wait and see.' She went into the house again and brought out the light wooden barrel and a thin, strong rope. She
5 handed the rope to Bond, lifted the barrel onto her back, and led the way along a path away from the village. The path descended slowly to a small, quiet bay in which a rowing-boat lay high up on the flat black stones. Bond pulled the simple boat down to the sea. He put in the rope and the wooden
10 barrel. Kissy went to the other side of the little bay and unfastened a string from one of the rocks. She began winding it in slowly and at the same time making a soft whistling sound. To Bond's amazement, a big black bird shot like a bullet through the shallow water and hopped up the beach to
15 Kissy's feet, moving its long neck up and down and making ssssss-ssss noises, as if in anger. But Kissy bent down and stroked the creature's head and neck, at the same time talking to it gaily. She came towards the boat, winding up the long string, and the bird followed in a clumsy way. It paid no
20 attention to Bond, but jumped untidily over the side of the boat, and climbed onto a small seat in the front, where it sat proudly. Occasionally it opened its wings to their full five foot width, with gentle grace. Then it finally settled down and stared out to sea with its neck coiled backwards like a
25 snake ready to strike, and its fierce green-blue eyes looking into the distance.

Kissy climbed into the boat and sat down. Bond took the heavy oars and began rowing at a powerful, even pace, more or less north, under Kissy's direction.
30 He had noticed that Kissy's line to the bird ended with a thin brass ring, perhaps two inches across, round the base of the bird's neck. So this was one of the famous fishing birds of Japan. Bond asked her about it.

Kissy said, 'I found him as a baby three years ago. He had
35 oil on his wings. I cleaned him and looked after him and put a ring on him. The ring had to be made larger as he grew bigger. Now, you see, he can swallow small fish, but he brings

the big ones to the surface in his beak. He hands them over
quite willingly and occasionally he gets a piece of a big fish as
a reward. He swims a lot by my side and stops me from feeling lonely . . . It can be very lonely down there, particularly
when the sea is dark. You will have to hold the end of the line   5
and look after him when he comes to the surface. Today he
will be hungry. It is three days since he went out, because my
father could not row the boat. I had to go out with friends.
So it is lucky for him that you came to the island.'

'So this is David?'   10

'Yes. I named him after the only man I liked in Hollywood.
He was an Englishman like you. He was called David Niven.
He is a famous actor and producer. Have you heard of
him?'

'Of course. I shall enjoy throwing this David a few pieces   15
of fish in exchange for the pleasure that the other David gave
me.'

The sweat began to pour down Bond's face and chest.
Kissy unfastened her scarf and leaned forward to wipe the
sweat away. Bond smiled into her dark eyes and saw, for the   20
first time, her small, straight nose and her flower-like mouth.
She wore no make-up, and did not need any. She had that
rose-coloured skin on a golden background — the colours of a
golden peach — that is quite common in Japan. Her hair, out
of its scarf, was black and thick. Her teeth were perfect. Her   25
arms and legs were long and she had a beautiful figure, equal
to any of the girls that Bond had seen in the dance halls of
Tokyo. But her hands and feet were rough with work, and
her finger-nails and toe-nails, although they were cut very
short, were broken. Bond found this rather charming. Ama   30
means 'sea-girl' or 'sea-man', and Kissy wore the marks of her
battles with the ocean. But her skin, in spite of its constant
contact with the salt water, glowed with health. But it was
her completely natural manner, her charming, direct smile,
that made Bond admire her so much. At that moment he   35
thought that there could be nothing more wonderful than to
spend the rest of his life rowing Kissy out into the distance

during the day and coming back with her to the small, clean house in the evening.

Don't be a fool, he told himself. Only another two days to the full moon, and then you'll have to get back to reality, to
5 the dark, dirty life you've chosen for yourself. He put the thought out of his mind. Today and the next day, he decided, were for him to spend with just Kissy and the boat and the bird and the sea. He must just make sure that they were happy days, and lucky ones for her and her sea-shells.

10 Kissy said, 'Not much longer. And you have rowed well.' She pointed to the right, to where the rest of the Ama boats spread out over the ocean. 'With us, it is "first come, first served" with the places that we choose. Today we shall row to a place that I know, and we shall have it to ourselves.
15 There the seaweed is thick on the rocks and that is what these shells feed on. It is about forty feet deep, but I can stay down for almost a minute. That is long enough to pick up two, even three shells if I can find them. That's just a matter of luck in feeling with the hands among the seaweed, for you
20 rarely see the shells. You only feel them, and you knock them away from the rock with the pick. After a while I shall have to rest. Then perhaps you will go down? Yes? They tell me you are a good swimmer. I have brought one of my father's diving-masks. You will perhaps not be able to stay
25 down very long to begin with. But you will learn quickly. How long are you going to stay on Kuro?'

'Only two or three days. I'm sorry.'

'Oh, but that is sad. What will David and I do for a boat-man then?'

30 'Perhaps your father will get better.'

'Perhaps. I must take him to bathe in hot mud at one of the volcanoes on the mainland. Otherwise I shall have to marry one of the men on Kuro. That is not easy. The choice is not wide and, because I have a little money from my film
35 work, and on Kuro a little money means a lot, the man might want to marry me for the wrong reasons. I shall hate that, but how is one to know?'

'Perhaps you will go back into films?'

Her expression became fierce. 'Never! I hated it. They were all disgusting to me in Hollywood. Nobody treated me honourably except this Niven.' She shook her head to get rid of her memories. 'No. I will stay on Kuro for ever. The gods will solve my problems,' she smiled, 'like they have today.' She looked at the sea ahead.

'Another hundred yards,' she said. She got up and, balancing perfectly in spite of the rough water, she tied the end of the long rope round her waist and fastened the mask above her forehead. 'Now remember, keep the rope tight and when you feel one pull, pull me up quickly. It will be hard work for you, but I will rub your back when we get home this evening. I am very good at it. I have had lots of practice with my father. Now!'

Bond pulled in the oars gratefully. Behind him, David began hopping from one foot to the other, stretching out his long neck. Kissy tied a short line to the wooden barrel and put it over the side of the boat. She followed it into the water. At once David dived. The line which Kissy had tied to the side of the boat began to move fast. Bond picked up the end of Kissy's rope and stood up. Kissy pulled down her mask and put her head under the water. In a moment she came up. She smiled. 'Yes, it looks fine down there.' She rested in the water and began breathing very deeply, with a soft whistling sound through almost-closed lips, to fill her lungs with air. Then, with a short wave of her hand, she put down her head and suddenly, like a white ghost, she was gone, straight down. Her feet moved behind her in a fast stroke to help the pull of the weights.

Bond kept an anxious eye on his watch. David appeared below him, holding a half-pound silver fish in his beak. Never mind the birds, thought Bond. This was no time to get mixed up with taking fish from the extremely sharp-looking beak. But, with a scornful glance, the bird threw the fish into the floating barrel and dived under like a black bullet.

Fifty seconds! Bond jumped nervously when the pull on

the rope finally came. He pulled it in fast. The white ghost appeared far below in the clear water. She came to the surface beside the boat and held up two big shells to show him. Then she dropped them into the barrel. She held onto the
5 side of the boat to get her breath back. She smiled up at him, began her deep breathing again to fill her lungs, and was gone again.

An hour went by. Bond got used to the work and had time to watch the nearest of the other boats. They covered per-
10 haps a mile of sea, and, from across the silent water, there came the whistle of the diving girls. The nearest boat rocked on the little waves perhaps a hundred yards away, and Bond watched the young man at the rope and caught an occasional sight of the girl, shining like a fish. He heard the excited chat-
15 ter of their voices. I hope I shan't disgrace myself when it comes to my turn to dive, he thought. Cigarettes and *sake* aren't a good mixture for this sort of work!

The pile of shells was slowly growing in the barrel and among them were perhaps a dozen leaping fish. Occasionally
20 Bond bent down and took one from David. Once he dropped a fish and the bird had to dive for it again. This time Bond received an even more scornful look from the green-blue eyes.

Then Kissy came up and climbed into the boat. She took off her mask and sat, breathing heavily, in the boat. Finally
25 she looked up and laughed happily. 'Twenty-one. Very good. Now take my weights and pick, and see for yourself what it is like down there. But I will pull you up in thirty seconds anyway. Give me your watch. And please do not lose my pick, or our day's fishing will be over!'
30 Bond's first dive was a clumsy one. He went down too slowly and barely had time to look at the sea-bottom. He had to admit to himself that his lungs were in very bad condition. But he had seen one likely rock, thick with weed, and on the next dive he went straight to it and held
35 onto it, searching among the roots with his right hand. He felt a shell there, but, before he could get the pick to it,

Kissy was pulling him up again. But he got the shell at his third try, and Kissy laughed with pleasure as he dropped it into the barrel. He managed to continue diving for about half an hour, but then his lungs began to ache and his body felt the cold of the October sea. 5

He came up for the last time at the same moment as David, who shot past him like a beautiful gleaming black-and-green fish. To show he approved, David pulled gently at Bond's hair as he dropped his fifth shell into the barrel.

Kissy was pleased with him. She had a rough brown towel 10 in the boat, and she rubbed him with it as he sat with bowed head and beating heart. Then, while he rested, Kissy pulled the wooden barrel in and emptied its contents into the bottom of the boat. She produced a knife and cut one of the fish down the middle. She fed the two halves to David, who was 15 swimming beside the boat in expectation.

Later they stopped for a lunch of rice with a few small bits of fish in it, and dry, salty seaweed. And, after a short rest in the bottom of the boat, the work went on until four o'clock, when a small cold wind came from nowhere and got between 20 them and the warmth of the sun. It was time to start the long row home. Kissy climbed into the boat for the last time and gave several gentle pulls at David's line. He came to the surface some distance from the boat, rose into the air and landed on the side of the boat. He went to his own seat, where he 25 stood with his magnificent wings stretched out to dry, and waited like a king for his boat-man to row him home.

Kissy wrapped herself in her brown towel and dried herself inside it. She announced that they had sixty-five shells, which was quite wonderful. Bond had brought up ten of these, 30 which was, she said, a very honourable first catch. Feeling pleased with himself, Bond fixed his eyes on the island which was now only a dot in the distance, and began to row towards it.

His hands were sore, his back ached as if he had been beat- 35 en with sticks, and his shoulders were beginning to feel the first signs of sunburn. But he comforted himself with the

thought that he was only doing what he had to do anyway —
getting ready for the swim and the climb, and whatever came
afterwards. Kissy's eyes never left him and the low sun shone
into them and turned their soft brown to gold. And the dot
5 became a lump, and the lump became an island, and at last
they were home.

14　The Six Guardians

The next day was as golden as the first. Their catch of shells went up to sixty-eight, mostly because Bond's diving was improving.

Bond wore a shirt to protect him from the sun. His catch of shells went up to twenty-one. The only black spot on his 5 day was the view he had of the black castle across the water and the big yellow and black warning balloon flying high above it.

During one of their rests, Bond asked Kissy what she knew of the castle. He was surprised to see the way her face dark- 10 ened.

'Todoroki-san, we do not usually talk about that place. It is almost a forbidden subject on Kuro. It is as if the devil himself suddenly made his home half a mile away across the sea from our home. And my people, the Ama, believe that 15 this is what has happened.' She didn't look at the castle wall, but pointed at it with her hand. 'Even the priest agrees with us. And already a story has grown up on the island. It says that our six Jizo Guardians will send a man from across the sea to kill this "King of Death", as we call him.' 20

'Who are these Guardians?'

'Jizo is the god who protects children. On the other side of the island, on the shore, there are five statues. The sixth has been mostly washed away by the sea. They are rather frightening to see. They sit there in a line. They have rough round 25 bodies of stone and round stones for heads. They wear white shirts that the people change every month. They have been there for centuries. They sit on the line of low tide, and, as the tide comes up, it covers them completely, and they keep watch over the surface of the sea and protect us, the Ama, 30 because we are "the children of the sea". At the beginning of every June, when the sea is warm after the winter and the diving begins, every person on the island joins a procession and we go to the Six Guardians and sing to them to make them happy and friendly towards us.'

'And this story of the man from Kuro. Where did it come
5   from?'

'Who knows? Perhaps from the sea, or the air. Where do stories like that come from? It is widely believed.'

'Not by me!' said Bond, and they both laughed and went on with their work.

10   On the third day, when Bond was sitting as usual, eating his breakfast on the door-step, Kissy came to the doorway and said softly, 'Come inside, Todoroki-san.' Puzzled, he went in and she shut the door behind him.

She said in a low voice, 'I have just heard from a messenger
15   from the priest that there were people here yesterday in a boat from the mainland. They brought presents — cigarettes and sweets. They were asking about the visit of the police boat. They said it came with three visitors and left with only two. They wanted to know what had happened to the third
20   visitor. They said they were guards from the castle, and that it was their duty to prevent unwanted visitors there. The old men of the village accepted the presents, but said they knew nothing. They told them to talk to the priest. *He* said that the third visitor was in charge of fishing licences. He had felt sick
25   on the way to the island and had perhaps been lying down in the boat on the way back. Then he sent the men away, and sent a boy to the top of the High Place to see where the boat went. The boy reported that it went to the bay beside the castle, and then back into the boat-house there. The priest
30   thought that you ought to know these things.'

She looked at him sadly. 'Todoroki-san, I feel very friendly towards you. I feel that there are secret things between you and the priest, and that they concern the castle. I think you ought to tell me enough to put me out of my unhappiness.'

35   Bond smiled and said, 'You are very beautiful and kind, Kissy. Today we will not take the boat out because I must have some rest. Lead me up to the High Place from which I

can take a good look at the castle, and I will tell you what I can. I was going to anyway, because I need your help. Afterwards, I'd like to visit the Six Guardians.'

Kissy collected their usual lunch in a small basket, and they set off along a small footpath up the hill behind the little grey village. Here there were occasional bushes of red and white flowers, and some trees which already wore their bright autumn colours. They came to the High Place, at the top of the thousand-foot hill. Bond told Kissy to stay out of sight while he went and stood behind the tall pile of stones at the top, and stared round it and across the water.

He could see over the high castle wall and across the park to the tall castle itself. It was ten o'clock. There were figures in blue working clothes with high boots and long sticks. They were moving busily about the grounds. They occasionally used the sticks to push them into the bushes, as if they were looking for something. They wore black masks over their mouths. Bond thought that perhaps they were doing the morning's rounds, looking for the night's suicides. What did they do when they found some poor, half-blind creature, or a pile of clothes beside one of the mud-holes? Did they take them to the Doctor? And, in the case of the living, what happened to them? And when he, Bond, climbed that wall tonight, where could he hide from the guards? Well, at least the sea was calm and it was cloudless weather. He was sure he could get there all right. Bond turned away and went back to Kissy. He sat with her on the thin grass. He stared across the harbour to where the Ama boats lay in the middle distance.

He said, 'Kissy, tonight I have to swim to the castle and climb the wall, and get inside.'

She nodded. 'I know this. And you are going to kill this man and perhaps his wife. You are the man who, we believe, had to come to Kuro from across the sea and do these things.' She continued to stare out to sea. She said sadly, 'But why did they have to choose you? Why not another, a Japanese?'

'Those people are foreigners. I am a foreigner too. It will

cause less trouble for the State if the whole matter seems to be merely trouble between foreigners.'

'Yes, I see. And has the priest given his approval?'

'Yes.'

5   'And if . . . And after. Will you come back and be my boatman again?'

'For a time. But then I must go back to England.'

'No. I believe that you will stay for a long time on Kuro.'

'Why do you believe that?'

10   'Because I prayed for it. And I have never asked for such a big favour before. I am sure the gods will do this for me.' She paused. 'And I shall swim with you tonight.' She held up a hand. 'You will need help in the dark and I know the currents. You could not get there without me.'

15   Bond took the small dry hand with its broken nails. His voice was hard. He said, 'No, this is man's work.'

She looked at him. The brown eyes were calm and serious. She said, and she used his first name, 'Taro-san, your other name means thunder, but I am not frightened of thunder. I

20   have made up my mind. And I shall come back every night at exactly midnight, and wait among the rocks at the bottom of the wall. I shall wait for one hour in case you need my help in coming home. These people may harm you. Women are much stronger in the water than men. That is why it is the

25   Ama girls who dive, and not the Ama men. I know the waters around Kuro as a farmer knows the fields around his farm, and I have as little fear of them. Please do as I ask. In any case, I shall hardly sleep until you come back. To feel that I am close to you for a time, and that you may need me, will

30   give me some peace. Say "yes", Taro-san.'

'Oh, all right, Kissy,' said Bond. 'I was only going to ask you to row me to a starting point down there somewhere.' He pointed to the left across the water. 'But if you insist on attracting the sharks . . . '

35   'The sharks never trouble us. The Six Guardians look after that. We never come to any harm. Years ago, one of the Amas caught her rope in a rock under the water, and the

people have talked about the accident ever since. The sharks just think we are big fish like themselves.' She laughed happily. 'Now it is all agreed and we can have something to eat and then I will take you down to see the Guardians. The tide will be low by then and they will want to inspect you.'   *5*

They followed another little path from the top. It went down to a small protected bay to the east of the village. The tide was far out and they could walk over the flat black stones and rocks. Here, on a stretch of flat, stony beach, five people sat on a square foundation of large rocks and stared   *10* out into the distance. But they weren't people. They were, as Kissy had described them, stone bodies with large round stones for heads. But rough white shirts were fastened round them, and they looked strangely human as they sat guarding the waters and what went on beneath them. Of the sixth,   *15* only the body remained. His head must have been destroyed by a storm.

They walked round in front of the five figures and looked up at the smooth, empty faces. Bond, for the first time in his life, had a sensation of deep religious feeling. He suddenly   *20* wanted to kneel and ask for their help in the work he had to do. He dismissed the idea, but he did bow his head and ask for good luck. He stood back and watched while Kissy, her beautiful face anxious, clapped to attract their attention and then made a long speech in Japanese in which his name came   *25* up several times. At the end, when she again clapped her hands, it seemed as if the round heads nodded. Of course not! thought Bond. But when they walked away, she said happily, 'It is all right, Todoroki-san. You saw them nod their heads!'   *30*

'No,' said Bond firmly, 'I did not.'

Later that night they crept round the eastern shore of Kuro and pulled the boat up between the black rocks. It was just after eleven o'clock and the giant moon rode high and fast through the high clouds. They talked softly, although   *35* they were out of sight of the castle wall and half a mile away from it. Bond carefully pulled on his *ninja* suit of black cot-

ton. It was comfortable enough and would give warmth in the water. He pushed the diving mask, which belonged to Kissy's father, up his forehead. The small floating container with his equipment floated behind him. He tied its string to
5   his right arm so that he would always know it was there.

He smiled at Kissy and nodded. Then she pulled down her mask and dived into the quiet, black-and-silver sea.

15   A Charming Place!

Kissy swam steadily and smoothly and Bond had no difficulty in following her busy feet as she crossed the narrow
strip of water. Soon they came to the huge wall. There were a
few untidy rocks at its base, but Kissy stayed in the water,
holding onto some seaweed in case a guard should see her in   5
the moonlight. But Bond guessed that the guards stayed out
of the park during the night so that the suicides could have
free entry. Bond pulled himself up on the rocks and unfastened the container. He took out the packet of climbing-irons.
He was ready to go. He waved at the girl. She replied with the   10
sideways wave of the hand that is the Japanese sign for 'goodbye', and then she was off across the sea again, a shining
white shape that was soon lost in the pale path of the moon
on the water.

Bond put her out of his thoughts. He was getting cold in   15
his wet black *ninja* suit and it was time to move. He examined
the giant stone blocks and found that the cracks between
them were quite wide, as in the case of Tiger's training castle,
and were big enough for a foot. Then he pulled down his
black mask and began to climb, pulling the plastic container   20
behind him.

It took him twenty minutes to cover the two hundred feet
of the slightly-sloping wall, but he only had to use his
climbing-irons twice when he came to cracks that were too
narrow to give a hold to his aching toes. And then he was at   25
one of the gun-openings. He slid quietly across the six feet of
flat stone and looked carefully over the edge into the park.
As he had expected, there were stone steps down from the
gun-opening. He crept down these into the dark shadows at
its base and stood up against the inside of the wall, breathing 30
heavily. He waited until he had got his breath back. Then he
slipped back his mask and listened. Not a breath of wind

moved in the trees, but from somewhere came the sound of
softly running water and, in the background, a regular, heavy
bubbling noise. The volcanoes and mud-holes! Bond, a black
shadow among the other black shadows, moved along the
5   wall to his right. His first job was to find a place to hide. He
needed a base-camp where he could shelter, and leave his container. He explored various trees and bushes but they were all
too well kept and there was nowhere to hide. And from
many of them came a sweet, poisonous night-smell. Then,
10 against the wall, he found a rough shed. Its door was half-
open. He listened and then gradually opened the door, inch
by inch. As he had expected, there was a dark pile of garden
tools, and the damp smell of such places. He moved with care
with the help of the rays of moonlight through the wide
15 cracks in the wooden walls. He got to the back of the hut
where there was a pile of used sacks. He thought for a moment, and decided that, though the guards would often visit
this place, it was still a useful base. He untied the cord of the
container from his wrist and began carefully moving some of
20 the sacks forward to provide a nest for himself behind them.
When it was finished, he hid his container and crept out again
into the park. He planned to make a first, quick exploration
of the whole place.

Bond kept close to the boundary wall. He slid like a dark
25 shadow across the open spaces between the bushes and trees.
Although his hands were covered with the black material of
the *ninja* suit, he avoided contact with the plants. These sent
out a continually changing variety of strong smells. From it
rose the thin cloud of steam which he remembered from the
30 photograph in the Chief of Police's office. As he stood and
watched it, a large leaf from one of the surrounding trees
came floating down and settled on the surface near him. At
once a dark shape swept down on the leaf from the water
around it, and immediately went down again. There was
35 some kind of fish in that lake, and not the kind that eats
vegetables. Only meat-eating fish would get excited like that.
Beyond the lake, Bond found the first of the mud-holes and

volcanoes, a bubbling pool of hot mud that moved constantly and sent up little fountains. From yards away, Bond could feel its heat. Evil-smelling steam rose and faded away towards the sky. And now he saw the hard outline of the castle, with its towers above the tree-line! Bond crept forward carefully,   5
waiting for the moment when he would step upon the noisy stones that surrounded it. Suddenly, through a belt of trees, he was facing the castle. He stopped in the shelter of the trees, and his heart beat fast.

Now he was close, the high black-and-gold building looked   10
taller than ever. Its curved, decorated roofs were like enormous wings against the stars. It was even bigger than Bond had imagined, with its supporting wall of black stone blocks. Bond thought about the problem of entry. Behind would be the main entrance, the low front wall and the open country-   15
side. But didn't castles always have a second entrance, low down, for escape? Bond crept silently forward. He put his feet down flat so that the stones hardly moved under them. At any moment he expected the white beam of a search-light or the yellow-and-blue flash of gun-fire. But he reached the   20
base of the wall without trouble and followed it along to the left. He remembered from ancient school lessons that most castles had an exit at the same level as the surrounding water.

And so it was with the castle of Doctor Shatterhand – a small, ancient door. Its iron-work was cracked and rusty, but   25
someone had fitted a new lock and chain on it. No moonlight reached this place. Bond felt carefully with his fingers. Yes! The chain and lock would yield to his tools from the secret pockets of his *ninja* suit. Would there be bolts on the inner side? Probably not, or there would not be a lock on the out-   30
side. Bond went softly back across the path, stepping careful-ly in his own foot-marks. I'll aim for that door tomorrow, he thought.

Now, keeping to the right but still following the boundary wall, he crept off again to explore. Once, something slid away   35
from his approaching feet and crawled into some fallen leaves. What snakes will really attack a man? Bond wondered.

Most snakes just go away if you disturb them. Do they hunt
by night or by day? . . . Bond didn't know. There were so
many dangers in Doctor Shatterhand's garden of death.
Bond was now on the same side of the lake as the castle.
5 He heard a noise and hid behind a tree. The distant crashing
among the bushes sounded like a wounded animal. But down
the path came a man, or what had once been a man. The brilliant moonlight showed a head which was swollen to the size
of a football, and only narrow lines remained where the eyes
10 and mouth had been. The man cried softly as he went along.
Bond could see that his hands were up to his swollen face. He
was trying to pull apart the swollen skin around his eyes so
that he could see out. Every now and then, he stopped and
let out one word in a terrible scream to the moon. It was not
15 a scream of fear or pain, but almost of prayer. Suddenly he
stopped. He seemed to see the lake for the first time. With a
terrible cry, and holding out his arms as if to meet a loved
one, he ran to the edge and threw himself in. At once the fish
came to the surface and the water bubbled with their move-
20 ment. A mass of small fish struggled to get to the man. Their
six-inch bodies glittered and flashed in the moonlight. The
man raised his head and gave a terrible scream. Then he went
under.
    James Bond turned away and wiped the cold sweat off his
25 face. Man-eating fish! Their powerful jaws and razor-sharp
teeth could tear the flesh from a horse's bones in less than an
hour! And this man had been one of the suicides who had
heard of this terrible death. He had come and searched for
the lake and had got his face poisoned by some pretty tree.
30 The Doctor had certainly provided a feast of death for his
victims!
    All right, Blofeld, thought Bond. That's one more reason
why I want to kill you! Brave words! Bond stayed near the
wall and kept going. Grey dawn was showing in the east.
35   But the Garden of Death had not quite finished showing
him what it could do.
    All over the park, a slight smell of burning hung in the air.

Many times Bond had to make his way around steaming cracks in the ground, or the bubbling mud of the mud-holes with their warning circles of white-painted stones. The Doctor was most careful in case anyone fell into one of them by mistake! But now Bond came to one which was the size of a 5 circular tennis-court. Here was a tiny temple in a cave at the back of it and − a pretty touch − a vase with flowers in it. Somebody had arranged them in a pattern which no doubt spelled out some perfumed message to anyone who understood Japanese flower-arranging. And opposite the cave, be- 10 hind which Bond lay hidden, a Japanese gentleman stood. He was watching the bursting mud-bubbles in the hot soup-like hole. James Bond thought he was a gentleman because the man was dressed in the top hat, long grey coat and black and white trousers of a high government official − or the father 15 of the bride. And the gentleman held a carefully rolled umbrella in his hands, and his head was bowed over it as if in prayer. He was speaking softly and quickly, like someone in church, either confessing or asking the gods for something.

Bond stood against a tree, hidden in the blackness. He felt 20 he should interfere, stop the man from doing this terrible thing. But how could he do so, knowing no Japanese, having nothing but his 'deaf and dumb' card to show? And it was important for him to remain a 'ghost' in the garden. He must not have stupid arguments with a man he didn't know, about 25 some ancient sin that he would never understand. So Bond stood, while the trees threw long black shadows across the scene. He waited, with a cold, stone face, for the man's death.

The man stopped talking. He raised his head and stared at the moon. He politely lifted his shining top hat. Then he re- 30 placed it, put his umbrella under one arm, and sharply clapped his hands. Then, walking calmly as if to a business meeting, he took the few steps to the edge of the bubbling, boiling mud-hole. He sank slowly in the sticky grey mud. Soon he was gone and only his grey top hat remained. Then 35 the hat slowly went down too, and a horrible smell of cooking flesh reached Bond's nose.

Bond tried not to feel sick. Here was one more victim for the garden of death. He was filled with hate. Why didn't the Japanese Air Force come and bomb this place, set the castle and the evil poison gardens on fire? How could this man con-
5   tinue to have protection from a small bunch of officials and scientists? And now here was he, Bond, alone in this dreadful place. He must try to do the job with almost no weapons except his bare hands. It was hopeless. He hadn't even one

chance in a million. Tiger and his chiefs were certainly asking a lot in exchange for their precious code machine!

Cursing his luck, cursing Tiger, cursing the whole of Japan, Bond went on his way. But a small voice whispered in his ear, 'But don't you want to kill Blofeld? Don't you want revenge for your wife's death? Isn't this a wonderful chance? You have done well tonight. You have got over his wall and explored. You have even found a way into his castle and probably up to his bedroom. Kill him in his sleep tomorrow! And kill her too, while you have the chance! And then, back to Kissy and, in a week or two, back over the North Pole in a nice comfortable aeroplane to London and a warm welcome from your chief! Come on! Get on with the job.'

And Bond listened to that inner whisper and went on round the last mile of wall and back to the gardeners' hut. He took a last look round before he went in. He could see the lake about twenty yards away. It was now dark grey in the approaching dawn. Some big insects were dancing in the softly rising steam. They were dragon-flies. Pink ones. But of course! The last words of Tiger's dying agent! That was the last horrible touch to this evil place. Bond went into the hut, picked his way carefully between the garden tools, pulled some sacks over himself and fell into a shallow dream full of ghosts and devils and screams.

16 Something Evil Comes this Way

The screams in his dream had become real ones when, four
hours later, Bond woke. There was silence in the hut. He
kneeled and looked through a wide crack in the wall of the
hut. A screaming man was running along the edge of the lake.
From his blue uniform Bond guessed he was a field worker. 5
Four guards were after him, laughing and calling as if they
were playing a game. They were carrying long sticks, and now
one of them paused and threw his stick after the man so that
it caught his legs and brought him crashing to the ground. He
got to his knees and held up his hands towards them, like a 10
beggar. The guards, still laughing, gathered round him. They
were short, powerful men in high rubber boots. They wore
black masks over their faces. They pushed at the man with
the ends of their sticks, and at the same time they shouted at
him in cruel voices. Then, as if at an order, they bent down 15
and each man took a leg or an arm. They picked the man off
the ground, swung him once or twice and threw him out into
the lake. The horrible silver fish swam towards the man. Now
screaming again, he beat at his face with his hands and tried
to swim for the shore. But his screams quickly became 20
weaker and finally they stopped as his head went down and
the red blood spread wider and wider on the water.

Laughing among themselves, the guards on the bank
watched the show. Now they were satisfied that the fun was
over, and they turned away and walked towards the hut. 25
Bond could see the tears of laughter shining on their cheeks.

He got back under cover and heard their loud shouts and
laughter only yards away as they came into the hut and
pulled out their gardening tools. Then they went off to their
jobs. For some time Bond could hear them as they called to 30
each other across the park. Then, from the direction of the
castle, came the deep note of a bell, and the men became

silent. Bond glanced at the cheap Japanese wrist-watch which Tiger had provided. It was nine o'clock. Was this the beginning of the official working day? Probably. The Japanese usually get to their work half an hour early, and leave half an 5 hour late, in order to gain the respect of their employers and to show their gratitude for their jobs. Later, Bond guessed, they would have an hour's lunch break, and work would probably finish at six. So he could have the grounds to himself only after half past six. Meanwhile, he must listen and 10 watch and find out more about the guards' duties. He had probably observed the first of these — finding, and killing, any suicides who had changed their minds during the night. Bond softly opened his container and took a bite at a piece of dried meat, and drank from his water-bottle. He wished he 15 could have a cigarette.

An hour later, Bond heard feet on the path on the other side of the lake. He looked through the crack in the wall. The four guards were standing in line like soldiers. Bond's heart beat a little faster. This looked like some sort of inspection. 20 Was Blofeld perhaps doing his rounds, getting his reports of the night before? Bond tried to see, but the trees were in the way. And then, following the path on the other side of the lake, two figures came into view. Bond's fists tightened with the excitement of seeing his enemy again. Blofeld, in his 25 gleaming chain armour and ancient steel helmet looked like something out of an old Japanese play. His right hand in its iron glove rested easily on a long naked sword. His left hand held the hand of his companion, a short powerful woman. An ugly bee-keeper's hat hid her face. It was made of dark green 30 straw with a heavy black veil hanging from it, down over her shoulders. But there could be no doubt! Bond had seen that square figure, now dressed in a plastic rain-coat above tall rubber boots, too often in his dreams. That was the woman! Irma Bunt!

35 Bond held his breath. If they came round the lake to his side, all he needed was one big push, to send the man in his armour into the water! But could the fish get at him through

the cracks in his armour? Unlikely! And how would he, Bond, get away? No, that was not the answer.

The two figures had almost reached the line of four men and at this moment the guards dropped to their knees, all together, and bowed their foreheads down to the ground. Then 5 they quickly jumped up and stood stiffly like soldiers.

Blofeld addressed one of the men, who answered very respectfully. Bond noticed for the first time that this particular guard wore a gun-belt round his waist. Bond could not hear the language they were speaking. It was impossible that 10 Blofeld had learnt Japanese. English or German? Probably German, as a result of some job in the war. The guard laughed and pointed towards the lake. There, a mass of blue clothing was moving softly up and down in the water, with the movements of the feasting fish inside it. Blofeld nodded, approving, 15 and the men again went down on their knees. Blofeld raised a hand to them and the couple moved on like a king and queen.

Bond watched carefully to see if the guards, when they got to their feet, showed any private expressions of scorn or of 20 laughter, once the master's back was turned. But there was no sign of this. The men hurried off to their duties with disciplined, serious looks.

Bond could see that Blofeld had the silent approval and sympathy of the Black Dragons. Blofeld told them to do the 25 things that Bond had watched only a few hours before. Blofeld had power from certain departments of State. He dressed for the part. People obeyed his orders. And the men had their job to do. *And* this was a powerful foreigner, who had strong influence in high places. And, if people wanted to kill them- 30 selves, why worry? If the Castle of Death, with perhaps an occasional extra push, was not possible, they would choose the railways or trams. Here was a public service. Almost a department of the Ministry of Health! So long as their masks protected them from the poisonous plants in the garden, the 35 main thing was to do their jobs with care, and perhaps, one day, they would get a Minister for Suicide appointed in Tokyo!

And now the two figures were coming back into sight, but this time from the left. They had gone round the end of the lake and were on their way back, perhaps to visit other groups of guards and get their reports. Tiger had said there
5 were at least twenty guards and that the park covered a large area. Five working parties of four guards each? Blofeld's face was covered and he was talking to the woman. They were now only twenty yards away. They stopped at the edge of the lake and looked, with curiosity, at the still-moving mass
10 of fish around the blue cloth. They were talking German. Bond listened hard.

Blofeld said, 'Those man-eating fish and the volcanoes are good house-keepers. They keep the place tidy.'

'The sea and the sharks are useful too.'

15 'But often the sharks do not finish the job. The spy that we put through the Question Room – they found him almost in one piece along the coast. The lake would have been a better place for him. We don't want that policeman from Fukuoka coming here too often. He may have ways of learning
20 from the local people just how many people are crossing the wall. There will be many more, nearly double the number that the ambulance comes for. If our score continues to increase in this way, there is going to be trouble. I see from the newspapers that Kono translates for me, that people are already
25 asking for a public inquiry.'

'And what shall we do then, dear Ernst?'

'Make the Japanese government pay us for what we leave behind, and move on. We can repeat the pattern in other countries. Everywhere there are people who want to kill
30 themselves. We may have to vary the attractions of the opportunities that we offer them. Other people have not the deep love of horror and violence that the Japanese have. A really beautiful waterfall, perhaps; or a bridge, or a cliff. Brazil, or somewhere else in South America might provide
35 such a place.'

'But the figures would be much smaller!'

'It is the idea that matters, dear Irma. It is very difficult to

invent something that is completely new in the history of the
world. I have done that. If my bridge, my waterfall, yields
only perhaps ten people a year, that is simply a matter of
figures. The basic idea will still be alive.'

'That is true. You are indeed a genius, dear Ernst. You   *5*
have already set up this place as a garden of death for ever.
People read about such things in stories, but no one has ever
made such a dream come true. It is as if one of the great fairy
stories had come to life. A sort of Disneyland of Death. But
of course,' she added quickly, 'grander and more noble.'   *10*

'In due course I shall write down the whole story. Then
perhaps the world will realize the type of man who has been
living among them. A man not only without honour among
his own people, but a man – ' Blofeld's voice rose almost to a
scream – 'whom they hunt down and wish to shoot like a   *15*
mad dog. A man who has to use every trick he knows, just to
stay alive! Why, if I had not hidden myself so well, there
would be spies on their way even now, to kill us both or to
hand us over for official murder under their stupid laws! Ah
well, dear Irma,' the voice was more normal, quieter, 'we live   *20*
in a world of fools in which true greatness is a sin. Come! It is
time to inspect the other guards.'

They turned away and were just preparing to continue
along the lake, when Blofeld suddenly stopped and pointed
like a dog directly at Bond. 'That hut among the bushes. The   *25*
door is open! I have told the men a thousand times to keep
such places locked. It is a perfect place for a spy to hide in. I
will make sure.'

Bond was afraid. He lay down and pulled the sacks over
himself to give extra protection. The loud iron steps ap-   *30*
proached and entered the hut. Bond could feel the man, only
yards away. He could feel the exploring eyes on him. There
came the noise of metal, and the wall of sacks shook at great
blows from Blofeld's sword. Then the sword crashed down
again and again. Bond bit his lip as the sword crashed across   *35*
the centre of his back. But then Blofeld seemed to be satisfied and the iron steps went away. Bond let his breath out

quietly. He heard Blofeld's voice say, 'There is nothing, but remind me to tell Kono about it tomorrow. He must clear the place out and put a proper lock on the door.' Then the sound of the steps went away, and Bond rubbed his aching back.
5   But, though many of the sacks above him were cut right through, his protection had been just deep enough and the skin across his back was not broken.

Bond got to his knees and put the sacks back. Then he spat the dust from the sacks out of his mouth. He took a drink
10 from his water-bottle and assured himself, through his crack, that there was no one outside. Then he lay down and let his mind wander back over every word that Blofeld had said.

Of course the man was mad. A year earlier, the usual quiet voice that Bond remembered so well would never have cracked
15 into that mad scream. And the coolness, the complete confidence that had always been behind his planning? Much of that seemed to have gone, perhaps, Bond hoped, partly because of the two great failures in his two most enormous plans. Bond had caused these failures, Bond and no one else.
20 But one thing was clear — Bond could not use the hut any more. Once again he thought over his plan. If he could get into the castle, he felt quite confident that he could find a way to kill Blofeld. But he was also fairly certain that he himself must die in the process — and at first he did not care
25 about that. But then he thought of Kissy, and he was not so sure about that. Kissy had brought a sweetness back into his life that he had thought was gone for ever.

Bond fell into an uneasy, watchful sleep that was once again full of creatures from the world of dreams.

17 Down the Hole

At six o'clock in the evening, the big bell rang again from the castle and it began to get dark. Insects sang like a tiny choir, and birds chattered in the bushes. The pink dragonflies went away and large frogs appeared in great numbers from their holes on the edge of the lake. As far as Bond could see   5
through his spy-hole in the hut wall, they seemed to be catching insects which were attracted by the shining pools of their eyes. Then the four guards came again, and there came the pleasant smell of a fire which, Bond supposed, they had lit to burn the rubbish which they had collected during the day.   10
Bond hid again as they brought their garden tools up the slope and put them away in the hut. They stood for a moment, chattering happily, and then, without noticing the untidy pile of sacks in the shadows, they went off in the direction of the castle.   15
After a short wait, Bond got up and stretched, and shook the dust out of his hair and clothes. His back still ached, but his main feeling was the desperate urge for a cigarette. All right. Perhaps it would be his last. He sat down and drank a little water and ate a large piece of his dried meat, then took   20
another drink from the water-bottle. He took out his single packet of cigarettes and lit one. He held the cigarette between his hands and quickly blew out the match. He breathed the smoke deep down into his lungs. It was wonderful! Another pull and the thought of his night's work seemed less frighten-   25
ing. It was surely going to be all right! He thought for a moment of Kissy, who would now be eating her vegetables and rice and fish, and preparing the night's swim in her mind. A few hours more, thought Bond, and she will be near me . . . But what will have happened in those few hours?   30
Bond smoked the cigarette until it burned his fingers, then put it out and pushed the cigarette end down through a crack

in the floor. It was seven-thirty, and some of the insect noises of sundown had stopped. Bond carefully made his preparations.

At nine o'clock he left the hut. Again the moon shone
5   down and there was total silence except for the distant bubbling of the mud-holes and the occasional chatter of a night bird from the bushes. He went the same way as the night before, came through the same line of trees, and stood looking up at the castle against the sky. He noticed for the
10 first time that the warning balloon with its advertisement of danger was tied to a pole at the corner of what appeared to be the main floor — the third, or centre, one of the five. Here, from several windows, yellow light shone faintly, and Bond guessed that this was where Blofeld was. He let out his
15 breath softly and walked off across the stony path. He came without trouble to the tiny entrance under the wooden bridge.

The black *ninja* suit was full of secret pockets. Bond took a tiny flash-light from one of them, and a small steel file. He
20 set to work on the chain that held the lock. Soon there came the final crack of parting steel. He bent the chain open and quietly removed the lock. He pushed lightly and the door opened. He took out his flash-light and stared into the darkness ahead of him with its thin beam. He was glad he did. On
25 the stone floor, where his first step would have taken him, lay a wicked man-trap. Its rusty iron jaws, perhaps a yard across, waited for him to step on the thin covering of straw that hid it. Bond felt sick as, in his imagination, he heard and felt the iron teeth bite into his leg just below the knee. Per-
30 haps there were other traps like this one — he must watch out for them!

Bond closed the door softly behind him, stepped round the trap and swept the beam of his torch ahead and around. Nothing but blackness. He was in some sort of large under-
35 ground cellar, where the owners of the castle had once stored supplies for a small army. Shadows swept across the thin beam of light, and he heard the squeaking of bats all around

him. Bond did not mind bats, or believe the old stories that
they got caught in people's hair. Their hearing was much too
good for that. He crept slowly forward, watching only the
rough stone floor ahead of him. Now the great cellar seemed
to become narrower, because he could see walls to right and   5
left of him, and above him an arched roof. Yes, here were the
stone steps leading upwards! He climbed them softly and
counted twenty of them before he came to the entrance. It
was a wide double door with no lock on his side. He pushed
gently and could feel and hear the resistance of a lock. It did 10
not sound strong. He took out a heavy tool and pulled until
there came the tearing sound of old metal and the noise of
nails or screws on stone. He pushed softly and, with a horribly
loud noise, the rest of the lock came away and half the door
swung open with a creak of old metal. Beyond was more   15
darkness. Bond switched off his torch, stepped through and
listened. But he was still deep in the cellars of the castle and
there was no sound. He switched his torch on again and saw
more stone stairs leading up to a modern door of polished
wood. He went up them and carefully turned the metal door   20
handle. No lock this time! He softly pushed the door open
and found himself in a long stone passage that sloped on upwards. At the end of it was another door, and beneath it
showed a thin strip of light!

Bond walked silently up the slope and then held his breath   25
and put his ear to the keyhole. Complete silence! He took the
handle and pushed the door open inch by inch. Then, satisfied, he went through and closed the door behind him. He
was in the main hall of the castle. The big entrance door was
on his left, and a well-used strip of red carpet stretched away   30
from it and across the fifty feet of hall, into the shadows that
the one oil-lamp over the entrance could not reach. The hall
was empty, except for the strip of carpet. There was still the
same smell of cold stone.

Bond kept away from the carpet and stayed in the shadows   35
of the walls. He guessed that he was now on the main floor
and that somewhere straight ahead of him was Blofeld. He

was well inside the castle. So far, so good!

   The next door, which must be the entrance to one of the public rooms, had no lock. Bond bent and put his eye to the key-hole. Another dimly lit room. No sound! He turned the
5 handle carefully, opened the door without a sound, and went through. It was a second huge room, but a rich and magnificent one this time. This was the main room, Bond guessed, where Blofeld received visitors. Between tall red curtains with gold edges, fine pieces of armour and weapons hung on
10 the white walls. There was a lot of heavy, ancient furniture arranged in groups on a huge central carpet of deep blue. The rest of the floor was of highly polished boards. They reflected the light from two great oil lamps which hung from the high roof. Bond, looking for places to hide in, chose the curtains
15 and, slipping softly from one hiding-place to another, reached the small door at the end of the room. This, he guessed, led to the private rooms.

   He bent down to listen, but immediately leapt for cover behind the nearest curtains. Steps were approaching! Bond
20 unfastened the thin chain from around his waist, wrapped it round his left fist, and waited, watching through a thin place in the curtain material.

   The small door opened half-way to show the back of one of the guards. He wore a black belt with a gun. Could this be
25 Kono, the man who translated for Blofeld? He had probably had a job with the Germans during the war. What was he doing? He appeared to be working with a piece of equipment behind the door. A light switch? No, there was no electric light. The man seemed satisfied. He backed out, bowed deep-
30 ly to someone in the next room, and closed the door. Bond caught a quick look at a narrow brown face as he passed Bond's hiding-place and walked across the room. Bond heard the sound of the other door and then there was silence. He waited at least five minutes, then he gently moved the cur-
35 tains to one side so that he could see across the room. He was alone.

   And now for the final stage! Bond kept his weapons in his

hands and crept back to the door. This time no sound came from behind it. Bond quietly but firmly pushed the door open and leapt through, ready to attack.

A completely empty, completely bare length of passage stretched perhaps twenty feet in front of him. A central oil *5* lamp gave a dim light and its floor was of the usual highly polished boards. A creaking floor like the one leading to Tiger's office? No. The guard's foot-steps had given no warning sounds. But from behind the door at the other end came the sound of music. It was Wagner, fairly loud. Thank you, *10* Blofeld! thought Bond. Most helpful! And he crept softly forward down the centre of the passage.

When it came, there was absolutely no warning. One step across the exact half-way point of the floor, and the whole twenty feet of boards slid silently away. Bond found himself *15* falling into black emptiness. The guard! The equipment behind the door! He had been setting the trap! In song and story, every castle had one, but Bond had forgotten. As his body dropped off the end of the sloping platform into space, an alarm bell rang. Bond had a quick impression of the plat- *20* form swinging back into position above him, then everything went black.

Bond swam up through the dark tunnel towards the blinding light at the end. Why don't they stop hitting me? he thought. What have I done to deserve it? Look, I have two *25* shells . . . He could feel them in his hands, rough and sharp at the edges. 'Kissy,' he said, 'stop it! Stop it, Kissy.'

The light grew and became a piece of floor covered with straw. He was lying on it while an open hand crashed sideways into his face. The pain was terrible. Bond saw the edge *30* of the boat above him. Desperate, he raised himself to catch at it. He held up the shells to show that he had done his duty. He opened his hands to drop them into the barrel. Then he realized where he was and he saw the two handfuls of straw fall to the ground. But the blows had stopped. And now he *35* could see, through a mist of pain. That brown face! Those narrow eyes! It was Kono, the guard. And someone else was

holding a torch for him. Then it all came back. No shells! No
Kissy! Something dreadful had happened! Everything had
gone wrong! Then realization swept through Bond's mind.
Careful, now. You're a deaf and dumb Japanese miner from
5   Fukuoka . . . The pain in your head isn't important. Nothing's
broken. Bond put his hands down to his sides. He realized for
the first time that he was naked except for his black cotton
ninja shorts. He bowed deeply and straightened himself.
Kono, his hand on his gun, spoke to him in angry Japanese.
10 Bond licked the blood that was running down his face and
looked as stupid as he could. Kono took out his small gun
and pointed. Bond bowed again, got to his feet, and, with a
quick glance round the straw-covered floor onto which he
had fallen, followed the guards out. There were stairs and a
15 passage and a door. Kono stepped forward and knocked.
    And then Bond was standing in the middle of a small,
pleasant room like a library. The second guard was spreading
out on the floor Bond's *ninja* suit and the contents of his
pockets. Blofeld, wearing a magnificent black silk robe with a
20 golden dragon across the chest, was leaning against the fireplace. The smooth, high forehead, the small purple mouth,
now with a dark-grey beard; the thick white hair, the black
eyes – Bond knew him at once! And beside him, completing
the picture of a couple at home after dinner, sat Irma Bunt,
25 in the dress of a high-class Japanese lady, with her sewing on
her knee. The square face, the brown hair and the thin, cruel
mouth; the light-brown, almost yellow eyes – there could be
no mistake! Yes, thought Bond, here they are! Within easy
reach! Was there still some way of getting at Blofeld? If only
30 the pain in his head would stop!
    Blofeld's tall sword stood against the wall. He picked it up
and marched into the middle of the room. He stood over the
pile of Bond's possessions and turned them over with the tip
of the sword. He picked up the black suit. He said in German,
35 'And what is this, Kono?'
    The head guard replied in the same language. His voice was
uneasy and his narrow eyes turned with a certain respect to-

wards Bond and then away again. 'It is a *ninja* suit, Doctor. These are people who practise secret arts. These arts are very ancient and I know little of them. They are the arts of moving silently, of killing without weapons. I did not know these
5   people still existed. Someone has certainly sent this man to murder you, my lord. If we had not set the trap, he might have succeeded.'

'And who is he?' Blofeld looked closely at Bond. 'He is tall for a Japanese.'

10   'The miners are often tall men, my lord. He carries a paper saying that he is deaf and dumb. And other papers, which appear to be in order. They say that he is a miner from Fukuoka. I do not believe this. His hands have some broken nails, but they are not the hands of a miner.'

15   'I do not believe it either. But we shall soon find out.' Blofeld turned to the woman. 'What do you think, my dear? You have a good nose for such things – a woman's approach.'

Irma Bunt rose and came and stood beside him. She looked carefully at Bond and then walked slowly around him, keep-
20   ing her distance. Then she said softly, 'My God!' She went back to Blofeld. She said in a whisper, still staring, almost with horror, at Bond, 'It cannot be! But it is!' She turned to Blofeld. 'This is the English agent. This is the man James Bond, the man whose wife you killed.' She added fiercely, 'I
25   swear it! You must believe me, dear Ernst!'

Blofeld's eyes were narrow. 'He looks like him, yes. But how has he got here? How has he found me? Who sent him?'

'The Japanese Secret Service. They will certainly have relations with the British Secret Service.'

30   'I cannot believe it! If that was true, they would have come to arrest me. There is too much in this business that we do not understand. We must be very careful and obtain the whole truth from this man. We must at once find out whether he is deaf and dumb. That is the first step. The Question
35   Room will settle that. But first of all we must soften him up.' He turned to Kono. 'Tell Kazama to get to work.'

18 The Question Room

There were now ten guards in the room. They stood in a line against the wall behind Kono. They were all armed with their long sticks. Kono shouted an order at one of them. The man left his stick in a corner and came forward. He was a great, box-like man with a hairless, shining head like a ripe fruit and *5* enormous, powerful hands. He took up his position in front of Bond. He spread his legs wide for balance. His lips drew back in a wicked smile of broken black teeth. Then he swung his right hand sideways at Bond's head and he hit him with great force exactly on the wound. Bond's head exploded with *10* fire. Then the left hand came at him and Bond staggered sideways. Through a mist of blood he could see Blofeld and his woman. Blofeld was merely interested, as a scientist, but the woman's lips were open and wet.

Bond took ten blows and knew that he must act while he *15* still had the purpose and the strength. The wide-open legs were the perfect thing to aim for. Through a red mist, Bond took aim and, as another giant blow was on its way, kicked upwards with every ounce of force. His foot crashed home. The man gave an animal scream and crashed to the ground, *20* rolling from side to side in his pain. The guards all rushed forward with their sticks ready, and Kono had his gun out. Bond leapt for the protection of a tall chair, picked it up and threw it at the angry crowd of guards. One of the legs caught a man in the teeth and there was the sound of breaking bone. The *25* man went down, his face in his hands.

'Stop!' It was the wild scream that Bond had heard before. The men stood still and lowered their sticks. 'Kono, remove these men.' Blofeld pointed down at the two wounded guards. 'And punish Kazama for his stupidity. Get new teeth for the *30* other one. And enough of this. This man will not speak with ordinary methods. If he can hear, the Question Room will get

the truth out of him. Take him there. The rest of the guards,
wait in the great hall. March!'
     Kono shouted orders to the guards. They marched away at
once. Then Kono opened a small door beside the bookcase
5   and pointed down a narrow stone passage. Now what? Bond
licked the blood from the corners of his mouth. He was very
weary. He could not take much more. And what was this
Question Room? Oh well, he thought, there may still be a
chance to get at Blofeld's throat . . . If only I can take him
10 with me when I die! He went ahead down the passage. He
was deaf to the order from Kono to open the rough door at
the end. The guard opened it for him, pressing the gun into
his back. Then Bond walked forward, into a strange room of
roughly cut stone that was very hot and smelt of burning.
15   Blofeld and the woman entered and took their places in
two wooden chairs under an oil lamp and a large kitchen
clock. The only unusual thing about it was that, at each quarter , there was a red line under the figures. The hands stood
at just after eleven and now, with a loud noise, the minute
20 hand moved. Kono signalled for Bond to come forward to
the far end of the room where there was a raised stone seat
with arms. It had grey mud on it, and there was the same vol-
canic mess on the floor all round it. Above the stone seat, in
the ceiling, there was a wide round opening through which
25 Bond could see a circle of dark sky and stars. Kono signalled
for Bond to sit down on the stone seat. In the centre of the
seat there was a large round hole. Bond did as he was told.
His skin felt the hot sticky surface of the mud. Tired, he
rested his arms on the stone arms of the seat, and waited. He
30 knew what this was all about and he was afraid.
     Blofeld spoke from the other end of the room. He spoke in
English. He said, in a loud voice that rang round the naked
walls, 'Commander Bond, or number 007 in the British Secret
Service if you prefer it, this is the Question Room, a trick of
35 my own invention that has the effect of making silent people
talk. As you know, this area has many volcanoes. You are
now sitting directly above one that throws mud, at a heat of

about one thousand degrees centigrade, a distance of about
one hundred feet into the air. Your body is now about fifty
feet above it. I had the charming idea of directing this volcano up a stone tube above which you now sit. This particular volcano erupts on exactly each fifteenth minute in   5
every hour.' Blofeld looked behind him at the clock. 'You
will observe that you have exactly eleven minutes before the
next eruption. If you cannot hear me, or the translation that
will follow, if you are a deaf and dumb Japanese miner as
your card says you are, you will not move from that chair. At   10
the fifteenth minute past eleven, you will suffer a most dreadful death by the burning of your lower body. If, on the other
hand, you leave the seat before the volcano erupts, you will
have shown that you can hear and understand. You will then
receive further treatment which will make you answer my   15
questions. These questions will discover who you are, and
how you come to be here; who sent you and with what purpose. You understand? You are sure that you do not prefer
to give up this play-acting? Very well. Just in case your papers
are partly correct, my chief guard will now explain the pur-   20
pose of this room in the Japanese language.' He turned to
Kono and spoke to him in German.

Kono had taken up his position by the door. He now
spoke to Bond in sharp Japanese sentences. Bond paid no
attention. He sat and stared calmly round the room. He had   25
remembered the volcanoes at Beppu and he was looking for
something. Ah, yes! There it was! A small wooden box in the
corner to his right. There was no key-hole to it. He was sure
that in it was the wheel to control the thing. Could he use
that bit of knowledge? Bond searched his tired brain for   30
some kind of plan. If only the terrible pain in his head would
stop! He rested his elbows on his knees and gently lowered
his hot face into his hands.

Kono stopped talking. The clock gave a deep iron tick. It
ticked nine times more. Bond looked up into the black-and-   35
white face. It said 11.14. A deep, angry growl came from
deep down beneath him, then a hard breath of very hot air.

Bond got to his feet and walked slowly away from the hole until he reached the area of the floor that was not wet with mud. Then he turned and watched. The growl had become a far-away roar. The roar became a deep howl that filled the
5 room, like a train coming out of a tunnel. Then there was a huge explosion and grey mud shot out of the hole. It shot through the opening in the ceiling. The fountain continued, absolutely solid, for perhaps half a second, and fierce heat filled the room. Bond had to wipe the sweat from his fore-
10 head. Then the grey fountain fell back into the hole and mud splashed down into the room in great steaming drops. A deep bubbling noise came up the stone tube and the room steamed. The smell of boiling mud was disgusting. In the total silence that followed, the tick of the clock to 11.16 seemed as loud
15 as a bell.

Bond turned and faced the couple under the clock. He said cheerfully, 'Well, Blofeld, you nasty little man, I'll admit that your stage-manager down below knows his job. Now bring on the dancing girls and if they're all as beautiful as Miss Bunt,
20 we'll set it to music and have it on the stage by Christmas. How about it?'

Blofeld turned to Irma Bunt. 'My dear girl, you were right! It is indeed the same Englishman. Remind me to buy you another string of grey pearls. And now let us finish with this
25 man for ever. It is past our bed-time.'

'Yes, indeed, dear Ernst. But first he must speak.'

'Of course, Irma. But that is no problem. We have already made him break his silence. The rest will be easy. Come!'

Back up the stone passage! Back into the library! Irma
30 Bunt went back to her sewing, Blofeld went back to his position by the fireplace. It was just as if they had returned after taking part in some graceful after-dinner entertainment. Bond decided, let's forget the miner! There was a writing-desk next to the book-shelves. He pulled out a chair and sat down.
35 There were cigarettes and matches. He lit a cigarette and sat back and enjoyed it.

Blofeld pointed to the pile of Bond's possessions on the

floor. 'Kono, take those away. I will examine them later. And
you can wait with the other guards in the great hall. Prepare
the equipment for further examination in case it is necessary.'
He turned to Bond. 'And now talk, and you will receive an
honourable and quick death by the sword. I am expert with   5
it and it is razor-sharp. If you do not talk, you will die slowly
and horribly and you will talk just the same. You know from
your profession that this is true. There is a degree of suffering
that no human being can bear. Well?'

Bond said easily, 'Blofeld, you were never stupid. Many   10
people in London and Tokyo know that I am here tonight.
At this moment, you might argue your way out of trouble.
You have a lot of money and you could employ the best
lawyers. But, if you kill me, you will certainly die.'

'Mister Bond, you are not telling the truth. I know the   15
ways of officials as well as you do. Therefore I dismiss your
story entirely and without hesitation. If my presence here
was officially known, a small army of policemen would already be here to arrest me. They might allow you to question
me after my arrest, but an Englishman would not have taken   20
part in the police action. It would be an American and Japanese matter.'

'Who said this was police action? When, in England, I
heard stories about this place, I thought the whole thing
smelt of you. I obtained permission to come and have a look.   25
But my chief knows where I am and, if I do not return, there
will be trouble.'

'That is not true, Mister Bond. Nobody will ever know that
you have seen me, nobody will ever know that you have been
here. I happen to have certain information that fits in with   30
your presence here. One of my agents recently reported that
the Head of the Japanese Secret Service, a certain Tanaka,
came down in this direction. A foreigner dressed as a Japanese accompanied him. I now see that your appearance is
similar to my agent's description.'   35

'Where is this man? I would like to question him.'

'He is not here.'

'How helpful for you!'

A red fire began to burn deep in the black pools of Blofeld's eyes. 'You forget that it is not you who are asking the
questions, Mister Bond. It is I. Now I happen to know all
5 about this Tanaka. He is a very hard man, and I will make a
guess. It fits the facts. This man Tanaka has already lost one
senior agent whom he sent down here to check on me. You
were around, on some business concerned with your profession, perhaps. For a fee, or in exchange for a favour, you
10 agreed to come here and kill me. I do not know or care when
you learned that Doctor Guntram Shatterhand was in fact
Ernst Stavro Blofeld. You have your private reasons for want-
ing to kill me. I have absolutely no doubt that you kept your
knowledge to yourself and passed it to no one for fear that
15 the official action which I have described would take the
place of your private plans for revenge.' Blofeld paused. He
said softly, 'I have one of the greatest brains in the world,
Mister Bond. Have you anything to say in reply? As the
Americans say, "It had better be good".'
20 Bond took another cigarette and lit it. He said calmly, 'I
stick to the truth, Blofeld. If anything happens to me, you,
and probably the woman as well, will be dead by Christmas.'

'All right, Mister Bond. But I am so sure of my facts that I
am now going to kill you with my own hands and get rid of
25 your body at once. In fact I prefer to do it myself, rather
than have the guards do it slowly. You have been a nuisance
to me for too long. The business I have to settle with you is a
personal one. My fine sword has not yet killed anyone. You
will be the first.' He turned to Irma Bunt. 'You agree, my
30 dear?'

The square face looked up from the sewing. 'But of course,
dear Ernst. What you decide is always correct. But be careful.
This animal is dangerous.'

19 Blood and Thunder

Bond dropped his lighted cigarette and left it to burn on the carpet. His whole body tightened. He said, 'I suppose you know you're both mad.'

'So was Frederick the Great, so was Van Gogh. We are in good, in famous company, Mister Bond. But what are you? You are just a common spy, an instrument for important men to use. Having done what they tell you to do, out of some mistaken idea of duty, or love for your country, you wait for your chiefs to send you on the next foolish adventure. Twice before, your chief has sent you to do battle with me, Mister Bond, and, by a combination of luck and force, you were successful. You and your government would consider these ideas as crimes against mankind. Various authorities are still trying to bring me to justice for them. But try to see these things as *I* do.'

Blofeld was a big man, perhaps six foot three, and powerful. He placed the tip of his sword between his wide-open legs and rested his thin, powerful hands on it. Looking up at him from across the room, Bond had to admit that there was something larger than life in the tall, proud figure, the direct stare of the eyes and the cruel thin lips. The Japanese robe, which they designed to make a race of small men look bigger, made something huge out of Blofeld's tall figure.

Blofeld paused. Waiting for him to continue, Bond took the measure of his enemy. He knew what was coming — excuses. It was always the same. When they thought they had got you where they wanted you, they tried to excuse their behaviour. Bond had seen it all before.

The tone of voice was reasonable, 'And so, Mister Bond, I came to invent this useful plan — the offer of free death to those who want to escape from the burden of being alive. I have provided the common man with the answer to his prob-

lems, and I have also provided the Japanese government —
though they seem blind to my kindness — with a tidy place
for this, instead of all those untidy suicides with trains,
trams, volcanoes and other unattractive, public methods of
5 killing oneself. You must admit that, far from being a crime,
this is a public service.'

'I saw your guards murdering one man yesterday.'

'Tidying up, Mister Bond. Tidying up. The man came here
wishing to die. What you saw was only helping a weak man
10 on his way. But I can see that you and I have nothing in common. I cannot reach what serves you for a mind. For your
part, you cannot see further than the simple pleasure of your
last cigarette. So enough of this idle chatter. You have already kept us from our beds far too long. Will you offer your
15 neck in an honourable way?' Blofeld took a step forward and
raised his huge sword in both hands and held it above his
head. The light from the oil lamps shone on the blade.

Bond knew what to do. He had known as soon as Kono
had led him back into the room. He had seen the wounded
20 guard's stick still standing in the corner. But there was a bell-
push near the woman. He must kill her first! Bond threw
himself to the left, took the stick and leapt at the woman just
before she could ring the bell.

The stick crashed into the side of her head and she fell off
25 the chair and lay still. Blofeld's sword whistled down, inches
from his shoulder. Bond rushed forward with the stick. The
tip caught Blofeld hard on the chest and threw him against
the wall, but he came forward again, swinging his sword.
Bond aimed at his right arm, missed, and had to retreat. He
30 was trying to keep his weapon as well as his body away from
the cruel steel. The sword, he knew, could cut the stick like a
match-stick, and its extra length was his only hope of victory.
Blofeld suddenly attacked, his right knee bent forward. Bond
jumped to the left, but he was too slow, and the tip of the
35 sword caught Bond's left side and drew blood. But, before
Blofeld could draw back, Bond had hit sideways at his legs.
His stick met bone. Blofeld cursed, and aimed a weak blow at

Bond's weapon. Then he came forward again. Bond made quick, short attacks to try to keep his enemy away. But he was losing ground in front of the fierce steel, and now Blofeld had victory in sight. He moved forwards, quick as a snake. Bond leapt sideways, saw his chance and gave a strong sweep 5 of his stick. It caught Blofeld on his right shoulder and made him curse again. His sword arm! Bond pressed forward, hit out again and again with his weapon. But one of his blows was too slow. Blofeld cut off a long piece of Bond's weapon. Blofeld saw his advantage and began attacking again. Bond 10 could only defend himself by hitting at the flat of the sword with his stick. But now the stick was slippery with the sweat of his hands. For the first time, Bond felt the cold breath of defeat on his neck. And Blofeld seemed to smell it, for he suddenly gave one of his fast, running lunges to get under 15 Bond's guard. Bond guessed the distance of the wall behind him and leapt backwards against it. Even so, he felt the sword-point close to his stomach. But he rushed forward again, flushed the sword aside with his stick and, dropping his weapon, made a dive for Blofeld's neck. He got both hands 20 round it. He pressed with his thumbs, and pressed and pressed. Blofeld's fingernails tore at Bond's face, trying to reach his eyes. Bond whispered through his teeth, 'Die, Blofeld! Die!' And suddenly the tongue was out and the eyes rolled upwards and the body slipped down to the ground. 25 But Bond followed it and knelt, his hands tight round the powerful neck, seeing nothing, hearing nothing in his wild urge for revenge.

Bond slowly remembered where he was. He removed his aching hands from around Blofeld's neck. Not looking again 30 at the purple face, he got to his feet. He nearly fell. How his head hurt! He tried to remember what he still had to do. He had had a clever idea. What was it? Oh, yes, of course! He picked up Blofeld's sword and sleep-walked down the stone passage to the question room. He glanced up at the clock. 35 Five minutes to midnight. And there was the wooden box, down beside the chair where he had sat. He went to it and

cut it open with one stroke of Blofeld's sword. Yes, there was the big wheel that he had expected! He knelt down and twisted and twisted until it was closed. What will happen now? he thought. The end of the world? Bond ran back up
5 the passage. Now he must get out, away from this place. But the guards were between him and the exit! He tore aside a curtain and broke a window with the sword. Then he looked around for something to cover his naked body. There was only Blofeld's magnificent robe. Coldly Bond tore it off the
10 body and put it on and tied the belt. The inside of the robe felt cold, like a snake's skin. He looked down at Irma Bunt. She was breathing heavily. Bond went to the window again and climbed out, taking care not to cut his feet on the broken glass.
15 He looked down. A hundred-foot drop to the path below! A soft whistle above him caught his ear. He looked up. It was only a breath of wind in the big notice under that stupid balloon! But then a crazy idea came to him, a memory of an old film. The gas balloon was strong enough to hold fifty feet of
20 cotton with the warning sign — was it powerful enough to take the weight of a man?
Bond ran to the window where the balloon's rope was attached. He tested the rope. It was as tight as a wire. From somewhere behind him there was noise and excitement. Had
25 the woman woken up and rung the bell? Holding onto the rope, Bond climbed out, cut a foot-hold for himself in the cotton notice, and took the rope in his right hand. Then he cut the rope from below, with Blofeld's sword, and threw himself into space.
30 It worked! There was a light wind and it blew him gently over the moon-lit park, over the glittering, steaming lake, to-wards the sea. But he was rising, not falling! The gas balloon was not at all worried by his weight! Then blue-and-yellow fire flashed from the upper floor of the castle and bullets
35 flew past him. Bond's hands and feet were beginning to ache with the effort of holding on. Something hit him on the side of the head, the same side that was already sending out its

message of pain. And that finished him. He knew it had! For
now the whole outline of the castle shook in the moonlight
and seemed to leap upwards and sideways and then slowly
dissolve like an ice-cream in the sunshine. The top floor fell
5   first, then the next, and the next. Then, after a moment, a
huge orange fountain of fire shot up towards the moon and a
breath of hot wind hit Bond and made the balloon shake.
There was a crack of thunder.

What was it all about? Bond didn't know or care. The pain
10   in his head was his whole universe. A bullet had hit the balloon, and it was fast losing height. Below, the softly swelling
sea offered a bed. Bond let go with hands and feet and fell
down, down towards peace, towards the feathers of some
childhood dream of softness and escape from pain.

20   An Announcement in *The Times*

The Times

Commander James Bond.

M. writes:

As your readers will have learnt from earlier reports, a
senior officer of the Ministry of Defence, Commander James   5
Bond, is missing, believed killed, while on an official mission
to Japan. I regret to report that we must now abandon all
hope of finding him still alive. It is therefore my duty, as
Head of his Department, which he served so well, to give
some account of this officer and his magnificent services to   10
his country.

James Bond was born of a Scottish Father, Andrew Bond,
and a Swiss mother, Monique Delacroix. His father worked
abroad and the boy's early education, from which he obtained a first-class knowledge of French and German, was en-   15
tirely abroad. When he was eleven years of age, both his
parents died in a climbing accident in Switzerland. The boy's
aunt, Miss Charmian Bond, became his guardian. He went to
live with her near Canterbury in Kent. There, in a small cot-
tage near the village green, his aunt, who must have been a   20
brilliant lady, prepared him for an English public school. At
the age of twelve he passed satisfactorily into Eton, the
school for which his father had entered his name at birth. I
must however admit that his time at Eton was short and,
after only six months, he left, as a result, I regret to say, of   25
some trouble with one of the servants. His aunt managed to
obtain a place at Fettes, his father's old school. There the
stricter way of life suited him. By the time he left, at the
early age of seventeen, he had twice fought for the school in
boxing competitions and had been a useful runner.   30

By now it was 1941 and, by saying he was nineteen, and

with the help of an old friend of his father's, he entered a branch of the Ministry of Defence. He ended the war as a Commander. It was about this time that I began my association with the Ministry's work, and it was with great pleasure 5 that I accepted Commander Bond's application to continue working for the Ministry in which, at the time of his sad death, he had risen to the rank of Principal Officer in the Civil Service.

The nature of Commander Bond's duties with the Ministry 10 must remain secret, but those who knew him will agree that he was a brave and good officer, in spite of a reckless side to his nature which occasionally got him into trouble with higher authority. He somehow managed to escape more or less unhurt from the many dangerous adventures into which 15 his duties led him. The reports which were made of some of these adventures, particularly in the foreign newspapers, made him, much against his will, something of a public figure. The result was that someone wrote a collection of popular books about him. If the quality of these books, or the truth 20 contained in them, had been any higher, the author would certainly have found himself in court under the Official Secrets Act. It is a measure of the scorn with which the Ministry regards these books that it has not taken any action against the author of these foolish stories of the adventures 25 of a magnificent public servant.

It only remains to me to assure his friends that Commander Bond's last mission was one of enormous importance to the State. Although, sadly, it seems unlikely that he will now return from it, I can announce on the highest authority 30 that the mission was one hundred per cent successful.

21　A Name from the Past

When Kissy saw the figure crash down into the sea, she sensed
that it was Bond. She covered the two hundred yards from
the base of the wall faster than she had ever swum before.
The tremendous fall into the water had at first knocked all
the breath out of Bond, but the will to live, which the terrible   5
pain in his head had almost destroyed, returned with the
shock of the cold water. When Kissy got to him, Bond was
struggling to get free from the robe.

At first he thought she was Blofeld and tried to strike out
at her.   10

'It's Kissy,' she said urgently, 'Kissy Suzuki! Don't you
remember?'

He didn't. He had no memories of anything in the world
except the face of his enemy and of the desperate urge to kill
him. But his strength was going and finally, cursing weakly,   15
he allowed her to get him out of the robe, and he listened to
the voice that spoke to him.

'Now follow me, Taro-san. When you get tired I will pull
you with me. We are all trained in such rescue-work.'

But, when she started off, Bond did not follow her. Instead   20
he swam weakly round like a wounded animal, in circles. She
almost cried. What had happened to him? What had they
done to him at the Castle of Death? Finally she stopped him
and talked softly to him. Like a child he allowed her to put
her arms round him and, with his head against her chest, she   25
set off.

It was an amazing swim for a girl – half a mile, against the
current, and only the moon and an occasional glance over her
shoulder to tell her where she was going. But she managed it,
and finally she pulled Bond out of the water in her little bay   30
and lay on the flat stones beside him.

She woke suddenly. Bond had been quietly sick and now

sat with his head in his hands, looking out to sea with the
blank eyes of a sleep-walker. When Kissy put an arm around
his shoulders he turned towards her. He looked confused.
'Who are you? How did I get here? What is this place?' He
5   examined her more carefully. 'You're very pretty.'

Kissy looked at him carefully. She suddenly had a brilliant
plan. She said, 'You cannot remember anything? You do not
remember where you come from?'

Bond passed a hand across his forehead. 'Nothing,' he said
10 wearily. 'Nothing except a man's face. I think he was dead. I
think he was a bad man. What is your name? You must tell
me everything.'

'My name is Kissy Suzuki and you are my boy-friend.
Your name is Taro Todoroki. We live on this island and we
15 go fishing together. It is a very good life. But can you walk
a little? I must take you home and get you some food, and
bring a doctor to see you. You have a terrible wound on the
side of your head and there is a cut across your chest. You
must have fallen while you were climbing the cliffs after
20 birds' eggs.' She stood up and held out her hands.

Bond took them and slowly got to his feet. She held him
by the hand and gently led him along the path towards the
Suzukis' house. But she passed it and went up the hill, to a
cave. It was large and the earth floor was dry. She said, 'This
25 is where you live. I live here with you. I had put away the
bed things. I will go and get them, and some food. Now lie
down and rest, and I will look after you. You are ill, but the
doctor will make you well again.'

Bond did as she told him and fell asleep at once, with the
30 unhurt side of his head resting on his arm. Kissy ran down
the mountain-side. Her heart was singing. There was a lot to
do, a lot to arrange, but now she had got her man back and
she was determined to keep him.

It was almost dawn and her parents were awake. She
35 whispered to them excitedly as she went about warming some
milk and putting together a roll of bedding, her father's best
robe and some of Bond's washing-things — nothing to remind

him of his past. Her parents were used to her little ways. Her
father merely commented mildly that it would be all right if
the priest agreed. Then, when she had washed the salt off
herself and dressed in her own simple brown robe, she ran up
the hill to her cave.   *5*

Later, the priest received her. He almost seemed to be ex-
pecting her. He held up his hand and spoke to the kneeling
figure. 'Kissy, I know what I know. The child of the devil is
dead. So is his wife. The Castle of Death is completely
destroyed. The man from across the sea did this, as the Six   *10*
Guardians told. Where is this man now?'

'In the cave. He is badly wounded. I love him. I wish to
keep him and care for him. He remembers nothing of the
past. I want it to remain like that, so that we may marry and
so that he may become a son of Kuro for ever.'   *15*

'That will not be possible, my daughter. In time he will
recover and go off across the world to where he came from.
And there will be official inquiries for him, from Fukuoka,
perhaps even from Tokyo, for he is surely an important man
in his own country.'   *20*

'But if you instruct the old men of the village, they will
tell these people that they know nothing. Then the people
will go away. All I want to do is look after him and keep him
for myself as long as I can. If the day comes when he wishes
to leave, I will not try to stop him. I will help him. He was   *25*
happy here fishing with me and my David-bird. He told me
so. When he recovers, I will see that he continues to be happy.
Ought not Kuro to take care of this hero whom the gods
themselves brought to us? Do not the Six Guardians wish to
keep him for a while? And have I not earned some small   *30*
reward for my humble efforts to help Todoroki-san and save
his life?'

The priest sat silent for a while with his eyes closed. Then
he looked down at the face at his feet. He smiled. 'I shall do
what is possible, Kissy. And now bring the doctor to me and   *35*
then take him up to the cave to see this man's wounds. Then
I will speak to the old men. But for many weeks you must be

very careful, and the foreigner must not show himself. When
all is quiet again, he may move back into the house of your
parents, and appear in public again.'

5   The doctor knelt beside Bond in the cave and spread out
on the ground a large map of the human head with the different parts marked with figures and Japanese writing. His
gentle fingers felt Bond's wounds, while Kissy knelt beside
him and held one of Bond's sweating hands in both of hers.
The doctor bent forward and, lifting the eye-lids one by one,

looked deeply into the empty eyes through a large reading-glass. On his instructions, Kissy ran for boiling water, and the doctor began to clean the cut which the bullet had made across the terrible swelling of the first wound, which Bond's
5 fall had caused. Then he covered the wound and tied up the head neatly. He put a bandage over the cut across the chest and stood up and took Kissy outside the cave.

'He will live,' he said, 'but it may be months, even years, before his memory returns. It is particularly the part of his
10 brain in which memories are stored that is damaged. For this, much education will be necessary. You will try all the time to remind him about past things and places. This will help him to remember.

'He ought to go to Fukuoka for an X-ray, but I do not
15 think anything is broken. In any case, the priest has ordered that he is to remain in your care, and his presence on the island must remain a secret. I shall of course obey the instructions of the honourable priest and only come to visit this man by different routes and at night. But there is much that
20 you will have to do, for he must stay very quiet for at least a week. Now listen carefully.' And the doctor gave Kissy detailed instructions which covered every point of feeding and nursing, and left her to carry them out.

And so the days ran into weeks. The police came again and
25 again from Fukuoka, and the official called Tanaka came from Tokyo, and a huge man, who said he was from Australia, arrived, and he was the most difficult of all for Kissy to send away. But the island of Kuro kept its secret. James Bond's body mended slowly and Kissy took him out for walks at
30 night. They also went for an occasional swim in the bay, where they played with David and she told him all the history of the Ama and of Kuro, and cleverly avoided questions about the world outside the island.

Winter came, and the Ama had to stay on shore and mend
35 their nets and boats and work in their vegetable gardens on the mountain side. Bond came back into the house and made himself useful with carpentry and other jobs, and learnt Japa-

nese from Kissy. The empty look left his eyes, but they remained very far-away, and every night he dreamed of a quite different world of white people and big cities and faces that he half-remembered. But Kissy assured him that these were just bad dreams and that they had no meaning. Gradual- *5* ly Bond came to accept the little stone-and-wood house and the endless sea as his own world. Kissy was careful to keep him away from the south coast of the island, and feared the day when fishing would begin again at the end of May. Then he would see the great black wall across the bay. Would it *10* bring his memory back?

Bond's lack of progress surprised the doctor. He decided that Bond's loss of memory was total, but soon there was no need for further visits because Bond's physical health and his complete satisfaction with his life showed that in every other *15* way he was completely recovered.

Winter slid into spring and fishing began again. Kissy dived again and Bond and the bird dived with her and there were good days and bad days. But the sun shone steadily and the sea was blue. Wild flowers covered the mountain-side and *20* everyone was very excited when the fruit-trees came into flower.

But one day, on the way down to their boat, Bond looked puzzled and asked her to wait before they put the boat out.

'I have something serious to talk to you about,' he told *25* her. Kissy's heart leapt and she sat down beside him on a flat rock and put her arms around him and waited.

Bond took a little torn piece of paper out of his pocket and held it out to her. She shook with fear and knew what was coming. She took her arms from round him and looked *30* at the paper. It was a rough square of newspaper.

Bond pointed. 'Kissy, what is this word "Vladivostok"? What does it mean? It has some kind of message for me. I connect it with a very big country. I believe the name of that country is Russia. Am I right?' *35*

Kissy remembered her promise to the priest. She put her face in her hands. 'Yes, Taro-san,' she said, 'that is true.'

Bond pressed his fists to his eyes and squeezed. 'I have a feeling that I have had a lot to do with this Russia, that a lot of my past life was concerned with it. Could that be possible? I want so terribly to know where I came from before I came
5   to Kuro. Will you help me, Kissy?'

Kissy took his hands from his face and looked at him. She said quietly, 'Yes, I will help you, my love.'

'Then I must go to this place Vladivostok, and perhaps it will awaken more memories and I can work my way back
10   from there.'

'If you say so, my love. The mail-boat goes to Fukuoka tomorrow. I will put you on a train there and give you money and full directions. I hear that one can go from the northern island, Hokkaido, to Sakhalin which is on the Russian main-
15   land. Then you can no doubt make your way to Vladivostok. It is a great port to the south of Sakhalin. But you must take care, for the Russians are not friendly people.'

'Surely they will not harm a poor fisherman from Kuro?'

Kissy's heart choked her. She got up and walked slowly
20   down to the boat. She pushed the boat into the water and waited for him to get in. James Bond took his place and took the oars in his hands. The bird climbed into its usual place. Bond measured with his eye the way to where the rest of the Ama boats floated on the water, and began to row.
25   Kissy smiled into his eyes and the sun shone on his back. So far as James Bond was concerned, it was a beautiful day just like all the other days had been, without a cloud in the sky.

But then, of course, he didn't know that his name was
30   James Bond. And, compared with the importance to him of that one Russian word on a little piece of paper, his life on Kuro, his love for Kissy Suzuki, were nothing.

Questions

Chapter 1 1. What game did Bond and Tiger play?
            2. Who was Tiger?
            3. Why was Bond uncomfortable?

Chapter 2 1. Why was M. worried about Bond?
            2. Why was Bond's secretary unable to call him when he was out?
            3. Where was Bond when the telephone call came?
            4. What excuse did Bond give M.?

Chapter 3 1. Why was Bond having to work under an Australian?
            2. What was his new number?
            3. What did Miss Moneypenny say to Mary Goodnight?

Chapter 4 1. Describe Dikko Henderson.
            2. Why didn't he like Tokyo?
            3. Why was Tiger seeing Bond so soon?

Chapter 5 1. Where was Tiger's office?
            2. What was the message that Tiger showed Bond?
            3. Why did Tiger let him pass it on to Britain?

Chapter 6 1. Why did Tiger call Bond 'Bondo-san?'
            2. Describe Tiger's room.
            3. What did Shatterhand describe himself as?
            4. What was special about the place he chose for his garden?

Chapter 7 1. Why was suicide important, according to Tiger, in Japanese life?
            2. What happened to the agent Tiger sent to the castle?
            3. Why was Tiger telling Bond all this?
            4. What did Bond say in reply?

Chapter 8   1. How did Tiger disguise Bond?
2. Describe the things in Bond's case.
3. What did Bond do wrong when he got on the train?
4. What was special about the lobster?

Chapter 9   1. What did Bond have to do at the temple?
2. What did the school they visited teach?
3. Who was following them?

Chapter 10   1. What did Tiger think of Bond's education?
2. What did Bond say about his own education?
3. What did Tiger say about the volcano?
4. What was special about *fugu* fish?

Chapter 11   1. What did Bond tell Tiger in the car?
2. Why did Bond's heart sink?
3. What was special about the people of Kuro?
4. Tell the story of Kissy's life.

Chapter 12   1. How did Bond get to the island?
2. Why were the people carrying blankets?
3. What did Bond's new name mean?

Chapter 13   1. What equipment did Kissy use in her work?
2. Who was David?
3. Why did she call him that?
4. How long could Kissy stay down under water?

Chapter 14   1. What was the story Kissy told Bond?
2. What did the priest do when the strangers came asking questions?
3. What reason did Bond give Kissy for Tiger deciding to send him and not a Japanese?

Chapter 15   1. How did Bond get into the grounds?
2. Where did he hide?
3. Why couldn't he stop the man from killing himself?

Chapter 16   1. Why did the Japanese arrive at work early and leave late?
2. Describe Blofeld and his wife, as seen in the garden.
3. How do we know Blofeld was mad?

Chapter 17   1. How did he get into the castle?
2. What happened to him in the passage?
3. What weapon was Blofeld holding?

Chapter 18   1. What did Bond do to Kono?
2. What was special about the Question Room?
3. How did Bond know the volcano was ready to erupt?
4. What did he say to Blofeld then?

Chapter 19   1. What weapon did Bond use against Blofeld?
2. Why did he hit the woman first?
3. Why did he put Blofeld's clothes on? How did he escape?

Chapter 20   1. Who were Bond's parents?
2. Why did he leave his first school?
3. How did he manage to join the Navy so young?
4. What did M. think of the reports in the papers?

Chapter 21   1. How did Kissy rescue Bond?
2. Why didn't she help him get his memory back?
3. Why did she cut all the English names out of the newspapers?
4. What word finally reminded Bond of his past?

OXFORD PROGRESSIVE ENGLISH READERS

GRADE 1

Vocabulary restricted to 1900 head words
Illustrated in two and partly in full colours
One illustration every 6 pages on average

The Adventures of Hang Tuah	MUBIN SHEPPARD
Alice's Adventures in Wonderland	LEWIS CARROLL
A Christmas Carol	CHARLES DICKENS
Don Quixote	CERVANTES
Great Expectations	CHARLES DICKENS
Gulliver's Travels	JONATHAN SWIFT
The House of Sixty Fathers	MEINDERT DEJONG
Islands in the Sky	ARTHUR C. CLARKE
Jane Eyre	CHARLOTTE BRONTË
Little Women	LOUISA M. ALCOTT
Madam White Snake	RETOLD BY BENJAMIN CHIA
Oliver Twist	CHARLES DICKENS
Plays for Malaysian Schools I	PATRICK YEOH
The Stone Junk	RETOLD BY D.H. HOWE
Stories of Shakespeare's Plays I	RETOLD BY N. KATES
The Tale of the Bounty	RETOLD BY H.G. WYATT
Tales from Tolstoy	RETOLD BY R.D. BINFIELD
Tales of Si Kabayan	MURTAGH MURPHY
The Talking Tree & Other Stories	DAVID McROBBIE
The Tiger of Lembah Pahit	NORMA R. YOUNGBERG
A Time of Darkness	SHAMUS FRAZER
Treasure Island	R.L. STEVENSON
Two Boxes of Gold & Other Stories	CHARLES DICKENS

GRADE 2

Vocabulary restricted to 2900 head words
One two-coloured illustration every 10 pages on average

The Adventures of Tom Sawyer	MARK TWAIN
Around the World in Eighty Days	JULES VERNE
Asia Pacific Stories	MURTAGH MURPHY
Chinese Tales of the Supernatural	RETOLD BY BENJAMIN CHIA
The Crocodile Dies Twice	SHAMUS FRAZER
David Copperfield	CHARLES DICKENS
Five Tales	OSCAR WILDE
The Hound of the Baskervilles	SIR ARTHUR CONAN DOYLE
The Missing Scientist	S.F. STEVENS
Plays for Malaysian Schools II	PATRICK YEOH
Robinson Crusoe	DANIEL DEFOE
Seven Chinese Stories	T.J. SHERIDAN
Stories of Shakespeare's Plays II	RETOLD BY WYATT & FULLERTON
A Tales of Two Cities	CHARLES DICKENS
Tales of Crime & Detection	RETOLD BY G.F. WEAR
Two Famous English Comedies	RETOLD BY RICHARD CROFT
Vanity Fair	W.M. THACKERAY

GRADE 3

Vocabulary restricted to 3500 head words
One two-coloured illustration every 15 pages on average

Animal Farm	GEORGE ORWELL
Battle of Wits at Crimson Cliff	RETOLD BY BENJAMIN CHIA
Dr Jekyll & Mr Hyde & Other Stories	R.L. STEVENSON
From Russia, with Love	IAN FLEMING
The Gifts & Other Stories	O. HENRY & OTHERS
Journey to the Centre of the Earth	JULES VERNE
Kidnapped	R.L. STEVENSON
King Solomon's Mines	H. RIDER HAGGARD
Lady Precious Stream	S.I. HSIUNG
The Light of Day	ERIC AMBLER
The Mask of Dimitrios	ERIC AMBLER
Moonraker	IAN FLEMING
The Moonstone	WILKIE COLLINS
A Night of Terror & Other Strange Tales	GUY DE MAUPASSANT
The Red Winds	SHAMUS FRAZER
Seven Stories	H.G. WELLS
Stories of Shakespeare's Plays III	RETOLD BY H.G. WYATT
Tales of Mystery & Imagination	EDGAR ALLAN POE
The War of the Worlds	H.G. WELLS
20,000 Leagues under the Sea	JULES VERNE
The Woman in White	WILKIE COLLINS
Wuthering Heights	EMILY BRONTË
You Only Live Twice	IAN FLEMING

GRADE 4

Vocabulary restricted to 5000 head words
One two-coloured illustration every 15 pages on average

Frankenstein	MARY SHELLEY
The Mayor of Casterbridge	THOMAS HARDY
Pride and Prejudice	JANE AUSTEN